Rethinking
Corporate Social Engagement

Rethinking
Corporate Social Engagement

Lessons from Latin America

LESTER M. SALAMON

Kumarian Press
An Imprint of Stylus Publishing

Rethinking Corporate Social Engagement

Published in 2010 in the United States of America by Kumarian Press, 22883 Quicksilver Drive, Sterling, VA 20166 USA.

The text of this book is set in 10.5/13 Palatino.

Editing and book design by Joan Weber Laflamme, jml ediset.
Proofread by Beth Richards.
Index by Robert Swanson.

Printed in the USA by Thomson-Shore. Text printed with vegetable oil-based ink.

∞ The paper used in this publication meets the minimum requirements of the American National Standard for Information Sciences—Permanence of Paper for printed Library Materials, ANSI Z39.48–1984

Library of Congress Cataloging-in-Publication Data

Salamon, Lester M.
    Rethinking corporate social engagement : lessons from Latin America / by Lester M. Salamon.
        p. cm.
    Includes bibliographical references and index.
        ISBN 978–1–56549–313–1 (pbk. : alk. paper) — ISBN 978–1–56549–314–8 (cloth : alk. paper)
    1. Social responsibility of business—Latin America—Case studies. I. Title.
        HD60.5.L29S35 2010
        658.4′08098—dc22

                                                                        2009046638

Contents

Illustrations

Acknowledgments

This book is the product of a body of research initiated at the behest of the Inter-American Foundation to determine the status and consequences of efforts it undertook beginning in the mid 1990s to encourage corporate engagement with grass-roots non-profit organizations in Latin America. I am indebted to David Valenzuela, then president of the Inter-American Foundation, for his foresight in promoting an inquiry of this sort and for his willingness to give me complete freedom to pursue the inquiry in a way I thought most effective. Thanks are also due to Pat Breslin and Paula Durbin of the Inter-American Foundation, who shepherded this study through its various stages with the same hands-off posture; to Larry Palmer, who took over the presidency of the Foundation when David Valenzuela left and supported the project's continuation in the same helpful manner; and to other staff of the Foundation for providing access to the Foundation's ample records on its efforts to encourage corporate social engagement in the region.

This study would also not have been possible without the aid of a team of local associates who provided expert reports on the corporate social engagement activities in their respective countries, and who set up the numerous interviews that form much of the core of the information on which this report relies. Included here are Professor Gabriel Berger of Argentina, Marcos Kisil of Brazil, Professor Ignacio Irrarázaval of Chile, Professor Roberto Gutiérrez of Colombia, and Klaus Gérman Phinder, Emilio Guerra Díaz, and Rosa Maria Fernandez of Mexico.

Also enormously helpful were three research assistants who played key roles in various aspects of the research: Bernard Brown, who undertook an exhaustive literature review on the context of corporate social engagement in Latin America and compiled important information from the files of the Inter-American Foundation; Alice Lariu, who compiled bibliographic materials on corporate social responsibility and pulled extensive data together on Inter-American Foundation support for corporate engagement activities in the Latin American region; and Jens Prinzhorn, who undertook a series of case studies in the five target countries examined here to verify and understand more fully a number of the examples of corporate activity uncovered in the course of the research.

Finally, I am grateful to the more than one hundred corporate social engagement officials and civil society leaders who graciously took time out of their schedules to talk with me about their work and their perceptions. They conveyed a refreshing sense of commitment and excitement about the tasks they have undertaken and the contribution they hope they are making to the quality of life in their region.

None of these individuals or organizations, or any others with which I am affiliated, bears responsibility, however, for the views or conclusions reached here or for the picture of the complex reality of corporate social engagement in Latin America that this book draws. That responsibility rests with me alone.

Abbreviations and Acronyms

ABRINQ	Association of Toy Manufacturers (Brazil)
AFC	Association of Oil Foundations of Colombia
AliaRSE	Alliance for Corporate Social Engagement in Mexico
AVAL	Administration by Values
BSR	Business for Social Responsibility
CEMEFI	Mexican Center for Philanthropy
CSE	corporate social engagement
CSO	civil society organization
CSR	corporate social responsibility
ExE	Empresarios por la Educación (Businesses for Education) (Colombia)
FECHAC	Chihuahuan Business Foundation
FEPIC	Fund for Training, Education, Prevention, and Community Integration
FSC	Forest Stewardship Council
GDFE	Grupo de Fundaciones y Empresas (Argentina)
GDP	gross domestic product
GIFE	Group of Institutes, Foundations, and Enterprises (Brazil)
GRI	Global Reporting Initiative
IAF	Inter-American Foundation
IDB	Inter-American Development Bank

IDEA	Institute for Enterprise Development (Argentina)
IDIS	Institute for the Development of Social Investment (Brazil)
ILSE	Latin American Institute for Educational Communication
IPD	Instituto para la Planeación del Desarrollo (Institute for Development Planning)
IPEA	Institute of Applied Economic Research (Brazil)
ISO	International Organization for Standardization
MEPE	Modelos Escolares para la Equidad (Model Schools for Equity) (Colombia)
NGO	nongovernmental organization
PDVSA	Petróleos de Venezuela
PNBE	Pensamento Nacional das Bases Empresariais (Brazil)
RS	Red Solidaria (Argentina)
SEDAC	Servicio para el Desarrollo, A.C. (Service for Development)
SENAC	Serviço National de Aprendizagem Comercial (National Commercial Training Service)
SOFOFA	Society for Manufacturing Promotion
WBCSD	World Business Council for Sustainable Development

Rethinking
Corporate Social Engagement

Chapter 1

Introduction:
A New Alliance for Progress?

*We propose to complete the revolution of the Americas, to
build a hemisphere where all can hope for a suitable standard of living and all can live out their lives in dignity
and in freedom.*
> —PRESIDENT JOHN F. KENNEDY

*Our final mission is social transformation. Business is just
a tool.*
> —ODED GRAJEW

In March 1961, President John F. Kennedy launched a bold new
initiative to alter longstanding American policy toward Latin
America by swinging it decisively behind the forces of reform in
the region. Among the ninety-four objectives outlined in the Char-
ter of Punta del Este that codified the resulting Alliance for
Progress were commitments to work with Latin American governments to promote more progressive tax structures, institute
meaningful land reform, democratize Latin governments,
strengthen civic organizations, and significantly reduce poverty.

Within a dozen years of its announcement, this bold Alliance
for Progress was officially disbanded, the victim of U.S. preoccu-
pation with the Vietnam War, growing authoritarianism in the
region, and changing electoral politics in the United States.

Three decades later, in August 1995, a small U.S. government
agency called the Inter-American Foundation (IAF) teamed up

with Fundación Social, an innovative Colombian social enterprise, to launch a new alliance for progress in the region, this one aimed not at the institutions of government but at two longstanding antagonists in Latin America's private sector: the business community and the growing network of NGOs that IAF had helped to foster in the region. The goal of this new alliance was no less ambitious, however; it was to mobilize the Latin American business community behind efforts being made by NGOs to alleviate poverty, protect the environment, and empower communities.

A little more than a dozen years after the Cartagena Conference that launched this new alliance for progress, its effort to stimulate greater social engagement on the part of Latin American businesses is not only alive and well but also has become something of a rage in the region. Newspapers and news magazines like *Exame* in Brazil and *La Nación* in Colombia issue regular rankings of corporate social responsibility performance, awards for exemplary corporate social engagement have proliferated, business schools have introduced courses on corporate citizenship, social impact reports have become *de riguer* components of corporate annual reports, staid institutions like the Inter-American Development Bank (IDB) have taken to staging elaborate corporate social responsibility conferences, and business leaders have begun portraying their enterprises not simply as business firms but as "cultural transformation agencies" promoting a "new ethic" of social and environmental "sustainability."[1] As one Latin observer put it: "It's hard for a company to avoid social responsibility [in Latin America] these days."[2]

How can we explain this striking development? What is the meaning of the apparent explosion of corporate social engagement in Latin America?

One part of the answer to this question, surely, is that the recent apparent surge in corporate social engagement in Latin America may really represent the rediscovery and repackaging of something that has been there all along. As two scholars have recently reminded us, Latin America has long been "a profoundly philanthropic region," reflecting the deep religious commitments of many of its leading business families.[3] What is more, there is a long tradition of innovation in business approaches to social issues in the region. Brazilian businesses, for example, took the initiative in the mid-1940s through their trade association, the

National Confederation of Commerce, to create an innovative network of commercial training centers supported by what was initially a self-imposed tax on corporate payrolls. This has since grown into a massive institution, SENAC, with seventeen regional affiliates and dozens of facilities.

Colombian businesses similarly established a self-taxing scheme in the mid-1950s to provide income support and related services to needy families. By 2004, the Cajas de Compensación Familiar had grown into a sprawling network of fifty-two institutions engaging close to 195,000 enterprises and providing a wide range of health and social services in addition to cash supplements and pensions to the families of needy workers.[4]

Colombia's Fundación Sociál is itself an innovative social institution, a *fundación propietaria,* or foundation in control of companies, an early example of what would now be termed a "social enterprise."[5] Created in 1911 by a Spanish Jesuit priest to organize women to teach children, Fundación Sociál owned nineteen commercial companies in construction, insurance, banking, leasing, and communications by 1997 and utilized the resulting profits to sponsor a host of philanthropic endeavors.

But *filantropia* in this region, while sizable and often innovative, has historically also been characterized by paternalism and *assistentialism.* As one pair of scholars has noted, "Such activities have long been oriented towards alleviating the suffering of select groups of the poor and downtrodden, but without aiming to address the causes of their poverty, or to transform an unequal and unjust status quo."[6]

So, too, it is quite possible that the recent "corporate social responsibility" craze in the region is merely a public-relations ploy. As two leading analysts of U.S. corporate social engagement recently acknowledged: "Increasingly, philanthropy is used as a form of public relations or advertising, promoting a company's image or brand through cause-related marketing or other high-profile sponsorships."[7] If this is true in the United States, once the epicenter of the corporate social responsibility (CSR) movement, is it possible that the Latin strain of the movement can have any more substance to it? Indeed, the organizers of a recent Inter-American Development Bank conference on CSR acknowledged as much when they noted that "on occasions, firms use the movement for corporate social responsibility as a defense mechanism against the criticisms from society of their irresponsible behavior."[8] The great challenge in assessing the recent surge of interest in CSR is therefore to get beyond the rhetoric, to focus on "deeds not words," as the IDB conference title put it.[9]

Purpose of This Inquiry

The aim of the present inquiry is to do precisely this, that is, to assess the current reality of corporate social engagement in Latin America. The impetus for the effort was an invitation from the IAF, the institution that helped plant and nurture some of the earliest seeds of the contemporary CSR movement in Latin America. After a decade and a half of investment in efforts to bring Latin American businesses into alliance with the grass-roots development organizations that have historically been the chief beneficiaries of IAF's activity in the region, IAF leaders wanted an assessment of how successful these investments have been and how meaningful the apparent growth of corporate social engagement in the region really is. In the course of carrying out this work, however, it became clear that the Latin American experience may hold important lessons for the corporate social responsibility field more generally, particularly in light of the economic crisis of 2007–9, which has put "the rich under attack," as a recent *Economist* headline put it.[10]

More specifically, this inquiry has sought to answer five basic questions about the recent experience with corporate social engagement in Latin America:

1. How real is the phenomenon of corporate social engagement and corporate–third-sector partnerships in Latin America? Has this phenomenon spread beyond a handful of firms and taken serious root in the region's businesses?
2. Why is this corporate social engagement happening? What goals are businesses pursuing through these efforts? What factors account for recent trends?
3. What forms are business social engagement and business–third-sector partnerships taking?
4. Are there noticeable variations in the patterns of business–third-sector partnership apparent among different countries or among different types or sizes of businesses?

5. What lessons, if any, does the recent corporate social engagement phenomenon in Latin America hold for other parts of the world?

Approach

Clearly, no single report can provide a comprehensive answer to these questions. Latin America is a huge and diverse region, and corporate social engagement takes myriad forms in the region's thousands upon thousands of enterprises. Indeed, it may even take different forms in the different components of an individual company. Like the elephant in the ancient tale, the nature of this beast will seem different depending on who touches it and where. Even with the best of intentions, the simplest of generalizations is therefore open to easy disproof. This is particularly the case given the limited systematic data available on this phenomenon in the region.[11]

To make sense of so complex and varied a landscape, it is therefore best to pursue a variety of routes, each of which can offer a unique perspective on the underlying reality, and then draw these together into a composite picture. This, at any rate, has been the approach utilized here.

More specifically, I have focused this inquiry on five countries widely acknowledged to represent different phases of the development of corporate social engagement in the region: Argentina, Brazil, Chile, Colombia, and Mexico. In each, I have pursued five different lines of work:

- **Literature review**—to tap into the extant literature on corporate social engagement and on recent social, economic, and political developments in the region.[12]
- **Interviews and field work**—to learn firsthand about corporate social engagement work in the five target countries from persons involved in the work as well as from government and civil society leaders affected by it. Close to one hundred such interviews were conducted.
- **Field reports**—prepared by local experts to tap into the best information and insights available in each country and ensure that my perceptions were rooted in a full understanding of local realities and available literature.[13]

- **Analysis of IAF grant records**—to take advantage of the unique insights into the emerging reality of corporate social engagement that these records contain.[14]
- **Case studies**—to follow up on the initial interviews and related material and delve more deeply into some of the interesting examples of corporate engagement uncovered through these other approaches.[15]

Evaluating Corporate Social Engagement: The Corporate Social Engagement "Pyramid"

Throughout this work my focus has been on what I term *corporate social engagement* or *business social engagement* rather than the much broader concept of *corporate social responsibility*. CSR, as it has come to be used, has taken on a wide assortment of different meanings—from abiding by the law, treating employees and business partners fairly, and avoiding or minimizing damage to stakeholders, to assuming a major share of the responsibility for promoting the welfare of society.[16] Reflecting this, the concept has expanded to a scale that would be impossible to portray for an entire region in any single report. Indeed, elaborate reporting systems replete with multiple indicators have been devised to capture the full scope of this phenomenon and a veritable cottage industry has developed to measure corporate performance in terms of them.

Brazil's Instituto Ethos, for example, divides corporate social responsibility into seven broad areas: (1) values and transparency; (2) work force; (3) environment; (4) suppliers; (5) consumers and customers; (6) community; and (7) government and society. Each of these is subdivided into subtopics, and each of the subtopics is defined in terms of a set of indicators. The "values and transparency" area, for example, is subdivided into two sub-areas ("self-regulation of conduct" and "transparent relations with society"), and these two are then further subdivided into five sub-sub areas. Just one of these sub-sub-areas—"ethical commitments"—is then measured in terms of seven indicators.[17]

While each of these areas and sub-areas is doubtless important, the focus here is on the aspect of corporate social responsibility that is perhaps of greatest public interest and that sets corporate social responsibility most clearly apart from other business concerns, namely, the assumption by businesses of a responsibility to the broader societies of which they are a part. This means their engagement in solving societal problems, such as the problems of poverty, lack of opportunity, inequality, inadequate education, and environmental degradation.

But what are the critical dimensions of such corporate social engagement and how can we tell whether the engagement is "real" and not just a public-relations effort? What criteria are most appropriate in assessing corporate social engagement?

While there are numerous answers to this question,[18] the dominant perspective in the field is what might be termed the "MBA approach" because it applies to the field of corporate social engagement many of the key ideas that form the core of modern business training more generally. More specifically, three basic ideas stand at the center of this corporate social responsibility approach.

The first, and most basic, of these ideas emphasizes that corporate social engagement is not just an ethical imperative, but also increasingly an economic one, that CSR pays off for businesses, and that there is therefore a compelling "business case" for it. As *The Economist* recently put it with characteristic sarcasm, "How wonderful to think that you can make money and save the planet at the same time."[19] The particular alchemy through which this transformation of social good into economic profit is supposed to be achieved differs somewhat among various advocates, however. For some, CSR allows corporations to avoid consumer boycotts or reduce the costs of capital. For others, it helps firms recruit and retain bright young workers and attract loyal customers. For still others, it allows firms to improve their "competitive context," that is, the quality of the inputs, product demand, legal environment, and supportive industries that critically affect their competitive position.[20]

Although this "business case" for CSR has not yet been reliably verified,[21] this has not prevented the mushrooming of CSR promotion efforts trumpeting the potential contributions of CSR to the ability of businesses to compete in the global marketplace, to attract and mobilize corporate staff, to promote a positive corporate brand image, to overcome popular alienation from big business, and thereby to secure a license for businesses to operate both in their home settings and in far-off lands. In the process CSR has won what *The Economist* has termed the "war of ideas." A recent Economist Intelligence Unit survey found that only 4 percent of business respondents thought that CSR was "a waste of time and money."[22]

A key facet of this developing business case for corporate social engagement is a second line of argument emphasizing the *multitude of stakeholders* that must be kept satisfied if businesses are to prosper. This includes not only stockholders interested in the return on their investments, but employees interested in the quality of their work environment and the broader *persona* of the firm for which they work, customers concerned not just about the quality of their purchases but also the image projected by the goods they buy, public officials whose opinions may well affect a corporation's ability to operate in a particular area, and the general public, whose attitudes may affect the leeway within which the business can function. Focusing exclusively on shareholders may consequently divert corporations from other stakeholders whose interests could have even greater impacts on the firm's survival and profitability and whose concerns relate as much to the corporation's social and environmental behavior as to its economic one.[23]

The third key concept that has formed the core of CSR doctrine is the idea that CSR must be "professionalized" and approached in a "business-like" fashion in order to be most effective. This means that the same techniques animating the business side of MBA training should apply to corporate social engagement as well, namely, a strategic perspective involving planning, targets, concrete impacts, and evaluation. Well-meaning charity is thus to give way to "strategic philanthropy," to approaches that adhere to clear social engagement strategies that are in sync with, and supportive of, the broader business strategies of the firms.[24]

Taken together, what I have termed the MBA approach thus suggests three indicators of the effectiveness of corporate social engagement either at the firm level or in countries and regions: first, its *proliferation* among firms and the recognition of this proliferation on the part of key stakeholders; second, the *professionalization* of this activity—its institutionalization, strategic focus, and integration with the broader business strategies of firms; and finally, its *profitability*, that is, its contribution to business bottom lines.

At least the first two of these criteria work well in the context of Latin America. Business social engagement, while hardly absent in Latin America, has historically been confined to a relatively narrow band of leading families controlling huge conglomerate family firms. As such, it has also tended to be highly personalistic and even paternalistic, in line with the broader clientilistic pattern of Latin American society.[25] Business families have provided Christmas baskets to workers in their firms, responded to personal appeals when illness or disaster strikes, and made contributions to the church and its array of social institutions. But this is a far cry from the broadened and systematized approach to corporate engagement advocated in the MBA approach. The spread of corporate social engagement to a broader set of firms and its institutionalization through regular procedures, guidelines, open application processes, and the like are therefore important markers of seriousness and progress even in Latin America.

At the same time, for all its strengths, in the context of Latin America and perhaps, following the economic crisis of 2007–9, in other regions as well, this MBA approach and the criteria that emerge from it still ring a bit hollow. This is so in part because attitudes toward the business community in this region are far more strident than in the United States or even Western Europe where the central CSR concepts were forged. Indeed, as will be noted more fully in Chapter 2, there is a long history of hostility to business among Latin American intellectuals and the public at large. The popular Latin American saying that "behind every fortune there is always a crime" is just one small indication of the atmosphere in which the business elite has long operated in this region.[26] Indeed, a deep social chasm separates the business elite from the poor in this region, and strong currents of resentment are not far from the surface, as the elections of Hugo Chavez in Venezuela and Lula in Brazil, not to mention the all-too-frequent kidnappings of corporate leaders, attest. However persuasive the "business case" for corporate social engagement is to the business community, therefore, its stress on the contribution such engagement makes to profits is a potential turnoff for other key elements in these societies, such as intellectuals, civil society groups, and sizable elements of the general public. It is well to remember, as *The Economist* reminded us in its recent special feature on CSR, that the important gift that corporations receive from the public sector in the form of their limited-liability legal status comes with a cost in the form of expectations that the corporations produce public benefits, and that cost has been rising everywhere, and perhaps nowhere more visibly than in Latin America.[27] Too utilitarian and self-serving an approach to social engagement can therefore backfire, intensifying suspicions rather than inspiring gratitude. Indeed, the continent is rife with suspicions of corporate intentions. As one Brazilian nonprofit leader explained:

> Corporate social responsibility is a new phenomenon in Brazil that has appeared and gained visibility at the same moment that neo-liberal economic policies have weakened social protections and globalization has begun to be criticized. This is not an accident. With business gaining enormous wealth while the poor were losing benefits, it became very important for corporations to develop a social face.[28]

What this suggests is not that the MBA approach is wrong in its assumption that there must be a payoff to social engagement for business. But in a context like the one that exists in Latin America, a context that may have become more common in the wake of the recent global financial meltdown, this approach may be insufficient. This suggests a need for other elements beyond those highlighted by the MBA approach for judging the seriousness, and potentially the effectiveness, of corporate social engagement in the Latin American context and those like it. More specifically, three other potential aspects of corporate social engagement loom larger from this perspective.

First is *participation*, the active engagement and empowerment of communities in the identification of corporate social engagement objectives and the design of social engagement initiatives. The MBA approach assumes that the task of formulating corporate social engagement strategies should be left fundamentally in the hands of business leaders and their consultants, who alone understand corporate business strategies and can therefore align corporate social engagement initiatives with them. The process is essentially inside out and top down, projecting priorities of the firm onto society. The role of communities in this model is essentially to accept what the corporations offer and express gratitude for it. None of the five steps recommended for the "new process" of strategic philanthropy recommended by Porter and Kramer— two of the most thoughtful exponents of the MBA approach— involves a significant effort to reach out to affected communities to identify their priorities and shape firm strategies around them.[29] To the contrary, while acknowledging that stakeholders' views are "obviously important," Porter and Kramer actually caution against too great a reliance on such views because "these groups can never fully understand a corporation's capabilities, competitive positioning, or the trade-offs it must make."

While this approach may help ensure the integration of corporate social engagement with corporate business strategy that is the MBA model's ideal, it seems likely to fall far short of winning corporations the support they need to prosper in a region such as Latin America, where suspicions about corporate intentions run deep and two decades of grass-roots organizing have awakened popular energies. For better or worse, the Latin American poor are demanding more of a say over the forces affecting their lives than the traditional MBA model seems to acknowledge, and populations in other parts of the world are likely not far behind.

Second is *partnering*. Whatever it does for companies, close observers of the corporate social engagement scene in Latin America are looking for evidence that corporations are seriously engaging the real problems of their region rather than pursuing cosmetic public-relations gambits. Since the problems are too enormous for any single company, or even any single sector, to handle on its own, one revealing indicator of the seriousness of corporate engagement is the extent to which companies enlist partners to gain meaningful traction on the problems they are addressing.

To be sure, some adherents to the MBA approach acknowledge the importance of partnerships as well. Porter and Kramer argue, in fact, that explicit partnerships are one way around the "free-rider problem" that can otherwise limit efforts to improve the competitive context that firms face. This problem arises from the fact that the improvements these efforts generate are available to competing companies in the same region, even if these companies do not help pay for them. This deters companies from making such efforts unless they can convince competitors to share the costs. As Porter and Kramer put it, "Philanthropy is amenable to collective corporate action."[30]

But the partnering considered crucial to local activists goes beyond corporate partnering with other companies; it focuses as well, and more centrally, on cross-sectoral partnerships forged with government and, particularly, with civil society. Such partnerships can root corporate engagement more deeply in social reality and give it greater thrust and reach, and therefore greater prospects for long-term success, than corporations could achieve on their own. It can also overcome the passivity and submissiveness that has long impeded progress in this region.[31]

Third, the active stakeholders evaluating corporate social engagement in Latin America know that the real payoff from corporate engagement comes not from what corporations do in society, but what they do in their businesses.[32] Despite the hype, the resources devoted to corporate social engagement are rather limited compared to the resources that companies utilize in their basic business operations. As David Vogel has noted: "One reason CSR often appears to 'pay' is not so much because its benefits are so substantial as because its costs have usually been modest."[33] What is important, therefore, is not simply the inside-out question of how corporate social engagement can be made to align with corporate business strategies, which is the focus of the MBA approach, but the outside-in question of how corporate *business* strategies and operations can be made to align with social engagement approaches and societal needs.

This point, too, has found reflection in at least some corners of the CSR movement. Indeed, a whole new vocabulary has surfaced to convey this concept, emphasizing not *corporate social responsibility* but *sustainability*. And an organization—the World Business Council for Sustainable Development—has been formed to advance it. But how fully this perspective has infiltrated the MBA approach to CSR is open to real question. In the context of Latin America, however, it is central to evaluating the seriousness with which corporations are approaching social engagement.

Finally, while the Latin American context suggests three additions to the list of criteria for effective corporate social engagement emphasized by the MBA approach, it also suggests the muting of one that has been central to that approach, that is, the emphasis on the contribution that CSR makes to corporate profitability. While this factor may be crucial to selling CSR to the Latin business community, it may have the precise opposite effect in selling the sincerity of corporate social engagement to the Latin American populace. Beyond that, however, a serious evaluation of this dimension falls well beyond the focus of this report, which is on the contribution that corporate social engagement is making to Latin American society rather than the contribution it is making to Latin American businesses. What is more, this dimension of corporate social engagement has already attracted considerable research. As summarized by David Vogel, this research reveals that:

> Unfortunately, there is no evidence that behaving more virtuously makes firms more profitable. . . . There is a business case for CSR, but it is much less important or influential than major proponents . . . believe.[34]

Taken together, therefore, this suggests five dimensions along which the movement toward effective corporate social engagement can be assessed: Proliferation, Professionalization, Partnering, Participation, and Penetration. These "five P's" define what might be termed the Corporate Social Engagement Pyramid, as depicted in Figure 1–1. While it is not quite the case that the levels of this pyramid represent stages of development that countries or individual companies must follow in any particular order, they do provide a workable framework in terms of which the evolution of corporate social engagement can be analyzed, mapped, and compared.

Put somewhat differently, these five dimensions define five processes of change that individual companies or entire countries must undergo in moving from traditional business philanthropy to effective business social engagement.[35] Thus, as reflected in Figure 1–2:

- *Proliferation* measures the extent to which corporate social engagement has moved beyond the narrow band of leading business families that tended to dominate traditional Latin American business philanthropy to engage the broader business community;
- *Professionalization* measures the extent to which the ad hoc and personal character of Latin American business philanthropy has been replaced by a more structured and more

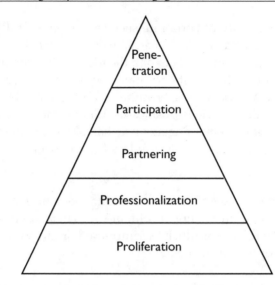

Figure 1–1. The Corporate Social Engagement Pyramid

permanent social engagement process, with dedicated staff, transparent guidelines, structured access points, and a strategic focus;

- *Partnering* measures the movement from the largely individualistic style of traditional business philanthropy, in which business leaders acted out of a personal sense of responsibility, often religiously inspired, but shied away from active engagement with other businesses or social institutions, except perhaps for the church, toward the more complex collaborative efforts, including collaborations with grass-roots nonprofit organizations, typically required to gain real traction on a country's social and economic problems;

- *Participation* measures the movement from a paternalistic style of business philanthropy toward a more progressive, empowering approach that engages those being helped as participants in the process in order to foster the more basic change required for real progress on longstanding social and economic problems; and finally

- *Penetration* measures the movement from the traditional practice of treating philanthropy as something essentially

Figure 1–2. The Corporate Social Engagement Pyramid in Action: Transforming Traditional Business Philanthropy into Progressive Corporate Social Engagement

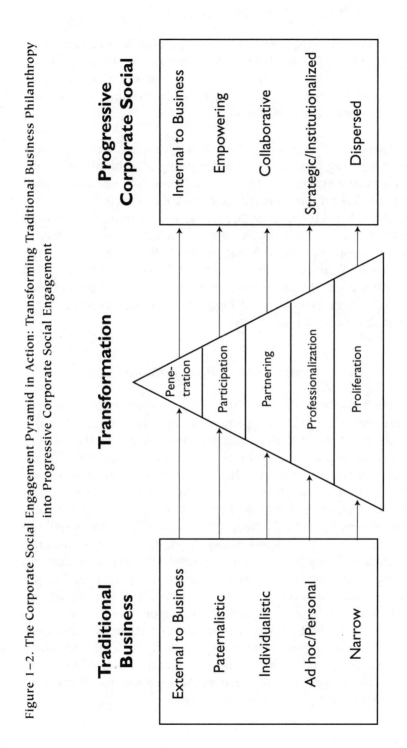

external to the firm to the more progressive practice of recognizing that the real test of corporate social engagement is the extent to which it animates a firm's *core business functions* (for example, its hiring processes, production processes, and supplier operations).

These five dimensions are not so much a refutation of the MBA approach as a broadening and deepening of it, highlighting elements that may be present in some manifestations of this approach but not given the emphasis and salience they deserve. Ultimately, as David Vogel reminds us, "CSR is sustainable only if virtue pays off."[36] But what it will take to "pay off" is heavily context specific, and that context is quite demanding in Latin America and growing more so in other areas as well. To achieve the "pay-off" of which it is capable, therefore, corporate social engagement may have to move its focus to the higher levels of the corporate social engagement pyramid.

Structure of Presentation

The balance of this book uses this framework to assess how fully corporate social engagement has met this broader standard in the five Latin American countries that have been the focus of my research. Given the multidimensional character of the framework, we should not expect that movement will be uniform along all five dimensions. Rather, particular countries, and even particular companies, may make progress on one or more of these dimensions but not on others. What is more, movement will not be unidirectional; progress along any of these dimensions, once made, can easily be reversed as a result of leadership changes, changing economic circumstances, corporate mergers and acquisitions, and many other factors. It is unlikely, therefore, that we will be able to reach a definitive conclusion about the extent to which the Latin American region, or even these five countries, have evolved a permanently dispersed, strategic, participatory, collaborative, and internalized form of corporate social engagement. But at least we will have markers to chart the dimensions of progress at a given point along the way.

Chapter 2 begins this process by assessing the extent to which business social engagement has *proliferated* in Latin America and how this proliferation process has unfolded. In addition, it seeks to examine some of the pressures and motivations that seem to be driving this process and to explain the notable variations that continue to exist from country to country.

Chapter 3 then turns to the degree of *professionalization* that has occurred in the corporate social engagement function in the region as reflected in the changing institutional structures for corporate social action and the efforts to forge more coherent, strategic approaches.

In Chapter 4 we take up the important question of the extent to which efforts are being made to build *partnerships* in addressing complex social and economic problems in the region, focusing particularly on partnerships between corporations and civil society and among businesses themselves.

In Chapter 5 we turn to the *participation* theme and the extent to which corporations are moving beyond the top-down and inside-out approaches to social engagement and are instead actively engaging communities in the design and execution of these activities.

Finally, Chapter 6 takes up the critical question of the extent to which social engagement is *penetrating* the business functions of the region's businesses as opposed to just their external philanthropic behavior.

What emerges from this review is an impression of a region whose business sector is in the midst of rather dramatic, and generally quite positive, change. The spirit of corporate social engagement has clearly caught hold in this region and is propelling some truly imaginative innovations. While critics will rightfully observe that the region's corporate social engagement glass is at best still half empty, they can nevertheless take heart from the realization that it is also getting close to being at least half full. Most important, perhaps, there is reason to believe that this new alliance for progress, whatever its exact form, has put down some solid roots. What is more, there is reason to believe that the style of corporate social engagement that is emerging in this region has important implications for companies elsewhere as well. A conclusion to this report draws these threads of observation together and suggests some crucial steps for the years ahead.

Chapter 2

Proliferation

The Spread of Corporate Social Engagement

> *There is a fire around us.*
> —MEXICAN BUSINESSMAN

In 1990, torrential rains caused severe flooding that devastated a large section of the city of Chihuahua, Mexico. In the face of this disaster, an unusual thing happened: a group of Chihuahua businessmen agreed to rally business support for a temporary tax on business earnings to finance recovery efforts if the state government would allow the businesses to administer the tax revenues themselves. Thus was born Mexico's first "community foundation," subsequently institutionalized as the Fundación del Empresariado Chihuahuense (the Chihuahuan Business Foundation—FECHAC) and financed by what ultimately became a permanent "community investment tax." Within a decade FECHAC had grown into a mature institution with forty-one professionals operating a micro-credit program and several other initiatives, and ultimately inspiring the creation of a similar nationwide business-sponsored community foundation called Fundemex.[1]

The story of FECHAC is emblematic of a new spirit that is animating the business community of Latin America. A new "cult of the *empresa*" has taken root in the region, a belief in the business firm as "the leading agent of social change," as one analyst has described it.[2] As the FECHAC experience demonstrates, this new spirit of business engagement is not limited to the capital cities or the large multinational firms, though they have clearly played an important role. Rather, bold business initiatives are springing up in unlikely places and in often-innovative forms.

To be sure, this is not the first time that Latin American businesses have pioneered novel commitments to social and economic problem solving. In addition to Brazil's SENAC and Colombia's Cajas de Compensación Familiar, cited earlier, there are multiple other examples. The Carvahal Foundation created by the Carvahal family in Cali, Colombia, in 1961 is one of these.[3] This foundation gained control at its founding of 35 percent of the stock of the Carvajal printing company, making it a rare breed in the region: a true, endowed foundation. But it then stepped out even more boldly into the political arena, spearheading a push for a national program of micro-enterprise development that led to the creation in 1984 by Colombia's government of the Corporación Mixta para el Desarrollo de la Microempresa (the Mixed Corporation for the Development of Microenterprise), and ultimately to US$7 billion in financing from the IDB for a comprehensive micro-enterprise development program.[4]

But against the background of a rather traditional, even paternalistic, pattern of business charity, as noted above, the new excitement evident in Latin American business circles is worthy of note, even if it remains embryonic in scope and uncertain in duration. Indeed, after lagging behind businesses in Europe and North America in promoting business social engagement, Latin American businesses appear well on their way to a great leap forward, forging their own "Latin style" of business social engagement that in many respects is more imaginative, more ambitious, more insistent, and, perhaps not unexpectedly, more passionate than its counterparts elsewhere.

The New Reality of Latin American Corporate Social Engagement

Solid data on this development is still, sadly, too sparse. But enough is available to make it clear that something significant, and potentially lasting, is under way. Consider, for example, the following:

- Five years after the introduction of the concept of corporate social responsibility in Brazil, a survey by the prestigious Instituto de Pesquisa Econômica Aplicada [Institute of Applied Economic Research—IPEA] revealed that 59 percent of all private companies, and 88 percent of all large companies (those with five hundred or more employees), were contributing to some type of social activity. IPEA researchers estimated the cumulative contributions of these companies at 4.7 billion Brazilian reals, or 0.4 percent of the Brazilian gross domestic product—four times the 0.1 percent of GDP that U.S. companies contributed as of 2005.[5]

- Four years later, IPEA researchers found that the proportion of companies addressing community needs had climbed from 59 to 69 percent, with much of the growth occurring among small- and medium-sized firms;[6]

- At least twenty institutions are actively involved in promoting corporate social responsibility in Brazil. These include early entrants such as the American Chamber of Commerce of São Paulo, which established an Eco award in the 1980s; the Group of Institutes, Foundations, and Enterprises (GIFE), founded in 1995; the Brazilian Association of Toy Manufacturers' "Company Friends of the Child" and ABRINQ Foundation, established in the mid 1990s; the influential Instituto Ethos created in 1998; and the social project exchange, recently established by Bovespa, the Brazilian stock exchange.

- Instituto Ethos, the "grandfather" of CSR diffusion agents in Latin America, now boasts 1,250 members, up from the 11 that were present at the founding in 1998; and 600 companies now regularly complete Instituto Ethos's social responsibility report;[7]

- Research in Argentina finds that almost every leading company is involved in some kind of social action and that the majority of these firms have professional staff dedicated to community programs;[8]

- 270 Argentine firms have signed the Global Compact, a United Nations initiative seeking to mobilize business to advance the Millennium Development Goals;[9]

- Corporate social engagement in Argentina seems to have persisted, and perhaps expanded, during the country's economic crisis of 2000/2001. According to one study, nearly 90 percent of large firms and substantial majorities of small and medium firms established or maintained programs of social support through the crisis period and thereafter;[10]

- Corporate social responsibility training courses have sprouted in business schools throughout the region, creating what one school calls the "pedagogy of the oppressor" to inculcate future corporate moghuls with the precepts of social engagement;[11]
- Numerous conferences and seminars supplement such academic offerings. In Chile alone there were six significant conferences on corporate social responsibility in 2006 alone;[12]
- Not surprisingly, all of this activity has attracted media attention and a growing army of consultants. In Mexico, for example, there are now four magazines devoted to corporate social responsibility—*Ganar-Ganar (win-win), Gestión, Expansión,* and *Lideres Mexicanos.* Mainline news media have also become engaged. The widely known Mexican newspaper *Economista* publishes a special section each Tuesday on *responsibilidad social,* and *Reforma* publishes a page called *Contacto* through which individuals and companies can make contact with philanthropic institutions. *La Nación* in Argentina, *Exame* in Brazil, *El Mercurio* in Chile, and numerous others have been similarly seduced by the CSR appeal. Indeed, advertisements and special supplements trumpeting corporate social activities have become a new revenue source for many of these publications. In the process, corporate social engagement has become a growing public expectation.
- In classic corporate fashion, award programs celebrating notable corporate social initiatives have also proliferated. Mexico now sports at least eight such awards—the Mexican Center for Philanthropy's (CEMEFI) "Socially Responsible Enterprise Certificate"; the CSR Best Practice Award; the Association of Fundraising Professionals' Award for Manager of the Year; the Social Foundation's Award for Social Leader of the Year; Mexico United for Values's prize for the manager contributing the most to social causes; the Ministry of Labor's Family-Responsible Enterprise Award; the Ministry of Labor's "Inclusive Business Award"; and the Ministry of the Environment's "Clean Industry Certificate."[13]

Chile, a relative newcomer to the CSR movement already has five or six such award or certificate programs. Indeed, the number of prizes may soon outstrip the number of business leaders available to receive them.

To be sure, there are enormous variations in the scope and seriousness of this business social engagement phenomenon, and there are serious concerns about whether the reality measures up to the rhetoric and hype. Even in Brazil, the apparent leader of this activity in the region, the dominant forms of business engagement remain rather traditional—the distribution of food and other direct assistance to persons in the vicinity of the business. Elsewhere, developments have not proceeded very far beyond the public-relations stage. In Chile, for example, most business social engagement activity takes the form of sporadic grants, and much of the leadership of the movement remains centered in the Chilean subsidiaries of foreign companies. The budgets committed to corporate social engagement also remain highly limited in most places and corporations have increasingly turned to alternative modes of involvement through volunteer programs and in-kind gifts of company products.[14]

Still, there are enough examples of innovative and committed engagement in serious social and environmental problem solving on the part of Latin American businesses to convince even the most inveterate cynic not only that something quite significant is under way in this region, but also that it has reached a critical takeoff point into self-sustained growth. Consider, for example, the following:

- The more than one hundred Colombian companies that have formed the Fundación Empresarios por la Educación (The Business Foundation for Education) and committed themselves to a long-term effort to improve local primary and secondary schools in cooperation with civil society, public authorities, and local communities;[15]
- The Ortópolis Project of cement company Holcim in Brazil, which is revitalizing the City of Barroso through a bottom-up community planning process;[16]
- The work of the Brazilian cosmetics firm O Boticário in creating a bio-diversity training center in the Salto Morato Nature

Preserve and fostering an indigenous industry drawing on natural products of Brazil's rain forests to produce baskets used in O Boticário's shops around the world;[17]

- The work of mining company Minera Escondida to build schools and other public facilities in Chile's Antofagasta region;[18]

- The effort launched by Fomento Social Banamex at the behest of Vincente Fox, former Mexican president, to promote economic opportunity in fifty of Mexico's poorest regions through a grass-roots empowerment process carried out in cooperation with a local NGO based in the provincial town of Ixmiquilpan;[19]

- The creation by Mexico's Bimbo Bakery Company of Reforestamos Mexico to provide a permanent vehicle to help the country recover from a devastating spate of forest fires and protect the country's natural forest resources;[20]

- The formation by the Toy Manufacturer's Association of Brazil of a new type of "articulating entity," the ABRINQ Foundation, to push for public policies to protect the rights and well-being of children;[21]

- Gas Natural of Argentina's work to extend gas lines to disadvantaged squatter communities in order to bring them lower-cost fuel;[22]

- The Producer's Clubs established by Wal-Mart Brazil to give indigenous producers an opportunity to access the huge Wal-Mart supply chain both in Brazil and internationally.[23]

Explaining the Upsurge

How can we explain this striking upsurge of corporate social engagement in Latin America over the past decade and a half or so? And what accounts for the variations in this phenomenon that exist from place to place?

Clearly, it is not possible to formulate a full explanation at this point. The available data are too sparse, and it is too early to know how durable or meaningful the current trend will prove to be.

But enough is now known to venture an educated guess about at least some of the factors that seem to be at work. Broadly speaking, they fall into two major categories: *demand* factors and *supply* factors. On the *demand* side are changes in the social, economic, and political *context* that have substantially increased the pressures on Latin American businesses to respond. On the *supply* side is an important set of *diffusion agents* that have encouraged, and helped to shape, the business response. Taken together, these two sets of forces have unleashed a veritable revolution in Latin American business thinking and practice. Let us examine the demand-side factors first.

The Demand Side: The Changing Context

That a development as widespread as the recent growth of corporate social engagement could take place in a region as diverse as Latin America in so relatively brief a period is evidence that some profound underlying shifts must have taken place in the fabric of society in this region. What were these shifts and what implications did they have for Latin businesses?

Although the changes that could alter the demand for corporate social engagement in Latin America over the past quarter century or more have been numerous, for our purposes here they can be grouped conveniently under three main headings: neo-liberal economic policies, democratization and civil society development, and globalization.

Neo-Liberal Economic Policies

In the first place, Latin American society has been profoundly altered by the introduction into the region of the set of neo-liberal economic policies that gained ascendance internationally with the elections of Ronald Reagan and Margaret Thatcher in the late 1970s and 1980s. These policies fundamentally challenged the prevailing model of state-centered development that had dominated this region for at least three decades. Beginning in Chile in the 1970s, and later extending to most other countries of the region with the support of the United States Government and the international economic institutions it largely supported, Latin American governments undertook a massive project of privatization and debt reduction that transformed the structure of Latin American economies and altered existing government social policies.

Generally speaking, Latin American governments sold controlling blocks of formerly public enterprises to private owners. In many cases the principal beneficiaries of these sales were the same family enterprises that had long dominated the local business scene. But in many other cases the local family enterprises were joined by externally based multinational firms. At the same time, governments began cutting back on social protections in order to comply with International Monetary Fund and Inter-American Development Bank demands for budgetary stringency. The up-shot was growing inequality and social unrest. At one end of the social hierarchy the economic elite grew in scale and extended its economic reach, while at the other end droves of poor people fled the rural areas to occupy sprawling *favelas* in the region's increasingly congested megalopolises.[24]

In Brazil, for example, the world's eighth largest economy, fifty-four million people—over one-third of the population—were officially considered to be poor as of 1999, and twenty-three million of these were considered indigent.[25] This was due not so much to the lack of wealth in the country as to its maldistribution. The Gini index of income inequality puts Brazil near the bottom of countries in terms of the fair distribution of income. Indeed, by the early 1990s the top 1 percent of the country's population controlled a larger share of the country's income than the bottom 50 percent.[26]

Elsewhere as well, social conditions worsened. In response, violence escalated. In Colombia, for example, the homicide rate is seven times higher than in the United States. Nor was this just a product of the drug trade or the activity of rebels and right-wing militias. All types of crimes increased—and not just in Colombia. Increasingly, the economic elite found it necessary to retreat into walled residences in gated communities and to travel in decoy cars with armed guards.[27]

With government increasingly on the sidelines, these deteriorating social conditions increased the demands on corporations and businesses, the only apparent winners from the neo-liberal policy shift. By 2000, for example, a poll in Brazil found 83 percent of the population agreeing that "big companies should have some responsibility to help reduce the difference between the rich and the poor."[28] The situation facing Latin businesses thus went well beyond the need to improve *the competitive context* of particular firms recommended by leading advocates of the MBA model of social engagement, as detailed earlier. The whole system of firms was in crisis. As one observer put it, "Latin America is a time bomb."[29]

Not surprisingly, the companies closest to the violence—such as extractive industries operating in the rural areas, or firms in countries with widespread guerrilla activity—were the first to get the message and the first to respond. "The violence has caused businesses to think differently in Colombia," notes the executive director of Avina Foundation's Colombia operation. But farsighted business leaders in other countries understood the situation as well. "I had eyes and could see the Brazilian reality," noted Oded Grajew, founder of Brazil's Instituto Ethos and formerly director of its Association of Toy Manufacturers. "Something had to be done about it."[30] For those slower to understand, the election of Hugo Chavez in Venezuela provided an object lesson, and one that business leaders took to heart.

Democratization and Civil Society Development

A second profound set of changes propelling corporations to rethink their social obligations was the turn to democracy that swept the region beginning in the 1980s and into the 1990s following a period of harsh military rule in at least three of the countries under consideration here—Chile, Brazil, and Argentina—and rather conservative one-party rule in one other—Mexico.

"Turn to democracy" may be a euphemism for what really took place, however. A more accurate description might be a peaceful democratic revolution that succeeded at least in cracking, if certainly not displacing, what one student has termed the region's prevailing pattern of "social authoritarianism," its hierarchical structure of social relations that regularly transformed poverty and disadvantage into a political and social, and not just an economic, condition.[31]

What cracked the shell of this clientilist structure was the wide array of social movements and grass-roots organizations that surfaced in the region during the 1970s and 1980s, challenging the prevailing structures of power and opening new spaces for citizen involvement. This "associational revolution" was fueled by a variety of forces: middle-class intellectuals frustrated by the constraints of authoritarian political regimes and elite-dominated economic structures, liberal priests freed by the Second Vatican Council from the requirement to prop up conservative political forces and empowered to establish Christian base communities through which the rural poor could pursue economic opportunity, new communications technologies that made it far easier to nurture grass-roots energies, and external actors such as the Kellogg Foundation and the Inter-American Foundation that were committed to encouraging this grass-roots effort at self-help and participatory development and willing to invest resources to promote it.[32]

Together, these elements began to change the terms of debate in Latin American society, putting elites on the defensive and signaling a new commitment to social, political, and economic rights for those on the bottom of Latin American society. In many parts of the region, business groups resisted these popular stirrings and sided with the conservative regimes. This was the case until rather late in the process, for example, in Chile and also to some extent in Mexico.[33] But in a few countries, at least some elements in the business community joined forces with those pushing for social reform and democratization.

This was notably the case in Brazil, for example, where a progressive group of younger business leaders, many of them veterans of the abortive 1968 student movement against Brazil's newly installed military government, convened in the mid 1980s, as the military regime wound down its incursion into politics, to form a progressive business think tank, the Pensamento Nacional das Bases Empresariais (PNBE) or Business Base for National Thinking. Many of the current leaders of the corporate social responsibility movement in Brazil cut their teeth on social reform through the PNBE, including Oded Grajew, founder of Ethos Institute; Sergio Mindlin, current executive director of Telefonica Foundation; Guilherme Leal, CEO of Natura, a prominent socially responsible cosmetics company; Marcos Kisil, former regional director for the Kellogg Foundation in Latin America and now president of an NGO that provides technical assistance to companies implementing social engagement activities; and Ricardo Young, currently president of Ethos.[34]

PNBE and its leaders played a significant role in the debate leading to the constitutional reform of 1988 that set Brazil back on a course toward democratization. It supported the campaign that impeached President Fernando Collor de Melio on corruption charges, the first time ever in Brazil that popular forces had

ousted a government official. And, most important for our purposes here, it served as the launching pad for many of Brazil's
early business social engagement initiatives, such as the ABRINQ
Foundation, an offshoot of the Association of Brazilian Toy Mak-
ers, which rallied business leaders' attention to the need to improve the deplorable circumstances of millions of Brazilian
children; and the Ethos Institute, the first to raise the flag of corporate social engagement in Brazil in a serious and comprehensive way. This combination of pressure from below and support
from a progressive wing of the business community probably goes
a good distance toward explaining Brazil's advanced position
among Latin American countries in the development and proliferation of corporate social engagement.

Globalization

The third contextual factor helping to drive the demand for a
serious embrace of corporate social engagement in Latin America
was globalization, in particular the growing penetration into the
Latin American business sector of a host of multinational corporations. In part, this was a byproduct of the privatization process
stimulated by neo-liberal economic policies. When governments
put huge public enterprises on the auction block for purchase by
private investors, as they did extensively in all five of the countries under consideration here, local buyers often found it impossible to raise enough capital to pull off the deals. They therefore
often had to establish partnerships with outside investors, including multinational corporations operating in the affected fields.
As a consequence, new players entered the Latin American business scene, disrupting the monopoly of the established business
families and producing what one pair of authors has termed a
"transformation of the entrepreneurial map."[35] Between 1980 and
1996, for example, foreign direct investment in Latin America and
the Caribbean grew from 6.4 percent of GDP to 17.4 percent. In
some countries, such as Mexico and Chile, the growth was even
more dramatic, reaching 22.3 and 27.3 percent of GDP by 1996,
respectively.[36]

Many of these multinational companies had already imbibed
the precepts of corporate social responsibility, with its stress on
social engagement as a way to win political and popular support.
In many cases they had well-established structures and strategies

in place through which to pursue this enlightened agenda. CSR thus became a new part of the competitive environment in the region as the new multinationals turned to social involvement as a marketing and differentiation strategy for their brands.[37]

In some parts of the region the multinationals became the prime movers behind efforts to introduce CSR into the region, as indigenous firms, still imbued with older traditions, held back. As recently as 1996, therefore, a major analysis of Latin American businesses could still fault the region's dominant business families for failing to become more socially active as the state withdrew.[38] Almost all the companies that belong to Acción RSE, the major promoter of business social responsibility in Chile, for example, are multinationals, and there is a heavy multinational presence in the front ranks of active CSR firms in the other countries as well. Under the new pressures created by globalization, however, local companies have been obliged to embrace the new ideas or see their clientele, and their reputations, further undermined by the new competitors, something few of them can afford, given the negative attitudes and suspicions that have long characterized popular attitudes toward corporations and the entrepreneurial class in the region.

The Supply Side: Diffusion Agents

While social and economic conditions may have created a demand for expanded corporate social engagement, the demand factors were hardly sufficient on their own to ensure that corporations would respond in a socially engaged manner. The key to transforming possibility into probability was the emergence of a set of supply factors, most notably in the person of a network of CSR diffusion agents. As Felipe Agüero, a student of Latin American corporate philanthropy, has reminded us: "Philanthropy is nothing new for businesses in Latin America. What is new is the discourse of corporate social responsibility, and the flurry of initiatives undertaken under that concept, including the creation of organizations by business leaders with the specific purpose of advancing it."[39]

So far as the discourse is concerned, the heart has been the MBA conception identified in Chapter 1, with its emphasis on the business case for CSR, the need to connect to a broader set of stakeholders than a company's shareholders, and the emphasis on institutionalization and a strategic approach. These ideas have been trumpeted in high-profile conferences and small training sessions, in special newspaper supplements and company social reports. As the organizers of the Inter-American Development Bank's 2003 conference on corporate social responsibility put it:

> It is increasingly clear that there is a business case for Corporate Social Responsibility (CSR). . . . By showing that CSR makes good business sense, we hope to show that it should not be a cyclical concern, [but] rather form part of a long-term business strategy. . . . Only the business case is going to make CSR sustainable over the long run and . . . ensure it is not just a temporary fashion.[40]

These standard refrains of the MBA mantra have been joined in the Latin American context, however, by other lyrics reflecting the special circumstances of the Latin American situation. One of these grows out of the deeply rooted religious and ethical impulses that continue to motivate the older business families, leading to what one leading Brazilian business philanthropist termed a "do it but don't show it" approach to philanthropy. From 1989 to 1998, for example, Fundação Educar Paschoal, a creation of the Paschoal Group of companies, publicized none of its extensive work creating new materials for educating children in the principles of ethics and the importance of education.[41]

A second distinctive Latin refrain is a surprising sensitivity to participation by recipients in the social engagement discourse in the region, a reflection, perhaps, of the region's deep social cleavages, its resulting violence, and its recent history of popular social movements and grass-roots organization. The oil company Hocol thus boasts that it is "teaching the Constitution to the people" by calling the attention of residents in the areas in which it works to the provision in Colombia's progressive 1991 Constitution mandating the formation of democratically elected community-action boards and helping them put such boards into operation.

Finally, the corporate social engagement refrain in at least some parts of the region seems to have embraced a more holistic view of what corporations need to do in order to act responsibly in the context of Latin America. The discourse thus holds businesses to something closer to the broader standard of social engagement articulated in Chapter 1 above, applying corporate social engagement principles not only to corporate social engagement actions, but also to the core of internal business operations.[42]

This set of ideas—both the core of the MBA approach and the special strains evident in Latin America—has caught on extensively among Latin American businesses; however, the process has not been automatic. Although there is a long history of business philanthropy in the region, as we have seen, many businesses nevertheless remained largely isolated from the social reality or comfortable with an arms-length relationship with their region's many social problems. Others felt it unseemly to rest the case for what to them was a moral and religious imperative on narrow commercial grounds or worried that an emphasis on the business value of corporate social engagement could backfire. As of 2000, for example, 76 percent of Brazilian companies responding to an IPEA survey cited humanitarian reasons, many of them religiously based, as the reasons for their involvement in social activity. What is more, the MBA approach to corporate social engagement posed a challenge to the personal control that leading families were accustomed to exercising over charitable contributions, transforming this function into a more formal, bureaucratic process operated by trained professionals rather than well-meaning family members. Since philanthropy remained one of the few preserves in which leading families could still operate unfettered by intrusive professional managers, this added to the reluctance to embrace the new dispensation.

The key to moving the corporate social engagement agenda forward, therefore, and to giving it its special Latin "flavor," was the emergence of diffusion agents that could more actively, and more professionally, propagate the new ideas. Especially effective here were several organizations that emerged indigenously, such as Instituto Ethos in Brazil and CEMEFI in Mexico,[43] but other entities also played crucial roles, such as the press and a number of important external actors.

Instituto Ethos

Instituto Ethos is probably the most widely known and most highly regarded of the CSR diffusion agents in Latin America. The organization boasts 1,250 corporate members and manages an active program of CSR reports that now involves six hundred of these companies. As one respondent put it: Ethos "officialized" CSR in Brazil, making it "the thing to do for corporations that wanted to be considered progressive and responsive to the country's enormous social problems."[44]

The origins of Instituto Ethos are instructive on many different levels.[45] The organization emerged as a natural outgrowth of the progressive business response to the military dictatorship, authoritarian politics, and deteriorating social conditions that enveloped Brazil in the 1980s and 1990s, but this process was aided at critical moments by a variety of outside supports—the U.S.–based Business for Social Responsibility, the W. K. Kellogg Foundation, and the Inter-American Foundation, among others. Oded Grajew, the founder of Ethos and an early activist in the PNBE organization mentioned earlier, was a key player in this process. As the head of the Brazilian Association of Toy Manufacturers (ABRINQ), Grajew perceived the need for a mobilized business community to take an active lead in promoting social change. As a toy manufacturer, he naturally gravitated to the issue of children's health and safety, an enormous problem in Brazil, where countless episodes of violence against children and youth, an alarming mushrooming of street children, and growing evidence of child prostitution and child labor were capturing press and public attention. Grajew therefore formed the Board for the Defense of Children's Rights within ABRINQ and recruited a number of other business leaders in the PNBE group to join it. By 1991 this entity had evolved into a separate organization, the ABRINQ Foundation for Children's Rights.

The formation of this foundation became a turning point in business understanding of its social role in Brazil. Rather than aiding children directly through traditional grants, the ABRINQ Foundation conceived its role as the mobilizer of Brazilian society on behalf of children, with the business community functioning in the unlikely role of spear headers. The ABRINQ Foundation thus launched a host of innovative mobilization efforts—a

Children's Rights Contest to educate children about their rights, a partnership with a children's publishing firm to distribute ten million copies of a pamphlet on children's rights, the Prefeito Criança (child-friendly mayor) program to encourage mayors throughout the country to prioritize child welfare, and the Empresa Amiga da Criança (child-friendly companies) campaign to encourage businesses to combat child labor.

The ABRINQ experience was a natural incubator for a broader concept of corporate social engagement among this key group of progressive Brazilian business leaders. But it took a sabbatical tour that Grajew was able to take to the United States and Europe in 1997, a critical link to the San Francisco–based Business for Social Responsibility (BSR) that grew out of it, and a pivotal BSR meeting in Miami in 1997 to move the process to the next level, inspiring Grajew to return to Brazil to found a new organization, Instituto Ethos, in 1998 with the assistance of eleven other corporate leaders.

Instituto Ethos essentially took the message of the ABRINQ Foundation to a broader audience and set of issues. In the process it put a distinctive Latin stamp on the CSR movement and did so with enormous effectiveness. Ethos set its goal not only to promote corporate philanthropy or corporate social responsibility, but also to change the culture of the business community by inculcating a new cultural value: a sense of collective business responsibility for solving societal problems. To do so, it forged partnerships with journalists to promote special supplements on corporate social engagement, established prizes, promoted CSR courses in universities, and created assessment tools that made it possible to rank corporations in terms of their social engagement activities. Ethos's assessment tools were revolutionary, if not in the field generally, then certainly in Latin America. They changed the discourse of corporate philanthropy in Brazil, and to a certain extent elsewhere in the region, extending the borders of social responsibility back into internal business practices dealing with work force and suppliers, and outward to relationships with consumers, the community, government, and the environment.[46] As one observer put it, "The creation of Ethos was a landmark in this whole process. Ethos took a broader idea of social responsibility and made it the standard."[47] Especially effective was its strategic use of the media to establish a new popular expectation of socially responsible business behavior.

By 2003, 760 enterprises had joined the organization, and three years later the number stood at 1,250, with its influence felt by thousands of others. To the extent that corporate social engagement has blossomed in Brazil, Instituto Ethos deserves a significant share of the credit.

CEMEFI

CEMEFI, the Centro Mexicano para Filantropia or Mexican Center on Philanthropy, has played a similar role in the diffusion of corporate social engagement in Mexico, though the fragmentation of the business community in Mexico and the absence of the kind of concerted initiative by progressive business leaders to challenge authoritarian political structures that occurred in Brazil has kept the diffusion process in Mexico much more fragmented and challenging.

CEMEFI itself was largely the creation of one of Mexico's leading businessmen and philanthropists, Manuel Arango Arias, who took the initiative in the late 1980s to form an institution dedicated to promoting philanthropy in Mexico, particularly among corporations.[48] One of CEMEFI's early projects was the Look Out for Others Program, which sought to connect two major social actors—the citizenry at large, and the corporate community—to social causes. Though still inspired by a traditional philanthropic orientation, the project planted the seeds for a more structured corporate social engagement focus by encouraging companies to target their efforts at particular social causes rather than dispersing their donations.

By the late 1990s, however, CEMEFI had found its way to the CSR movement internationally. CEMEFI thus launched a CSR training program in Mexico in the late 1990s in cooperation with the UK-based Prince of Wales Business Leaders Forum. It then escalated its involvement by establishing a certification process for socially responsible companies. This process requires that companies report on some 120 indicators of social responsibility, ranging from working conditions within the company to corporate relations with the community and with the environment. Companies that pass muster on these indicators receive the CSE Distinction certification from CEMEFI. Seventeen companies were awarded this seal in 2001, and by 2006 the number had grown to 124, demonstrating the appeal that the CSE Distinction has for companies.

CEMEFI also launched an ambitious effort to promote the formation of community foundations throughout the country, drawing on the experience of the Chihuahua businessmen cited earlier. Within five years thirteen such foundations had been created, a number of them with endowments, a rarity in the Mexican foundation world.

Other Diffusion Agents

Instituto Ethos and CEMEFI are by no means the only active corporate social engagement diffusion agents in the region. To the contrary, both of them have helped spawn other diffusion entities and prompted existing business federations to take a more active role in promoting corporate social engagement themselves. In Mexico, for example, CEMEFI joined with several other organizations in 2001 to form the Alliance for Corporate Social Engagement in Mexico (AliaRSE). Administration by Values (AVAL), the Organization for the Promotion and Development of Social Responsibility, the Endeavor Alliance, the Consejo Coordinator Empresarial (Businessmen's Coordination Board), and numerous others have subsequently joined the process in the country.

The scope and scale of diffusion agents is more modest in other parts of the region, but hardly nonexistent. In Argentina, the Grupo de Fundaciones y Empresas (GDFE), started in 1995 by local corporate and private foundations and originally called the Grupo de Fundaciones, has carried the torch for CSR in that country along with several other organizations, such as the Argentine Institute for Enterprise Development (IDEA), the Argentine Business Council for Sustainable Development, and the Argentine Corporate Social Responsibility Institute.[49] In Chile, Acción RSE has carved out a similar function along with PROHUMANA.[50]

The emergence of these specialized organizations committed to corporate social engagement has helped to stimulate Latin America's traditionally strong business associations into action. The role of these organizations in the diffusion of corporate social engagement may, in fact, constitute another one of the distinguishing features of the corporate social engagement movement in this region. We have already seen, for example, the pivotal role that the Brazilian Toy Manufacturers Association played in the early history of corporate social engagement in Brazil, and similar instances are evident in other parts of the region as well. Thus, the association of paper manufacturers in Mexico took the lead in forming the Fundación Dibujando un Mañana (the Drawing a Future Foundation). The petroleum industry association in Colombia helped promote a new participatory style of corporate engagement with communities.[51] And Chile's Society for Manufacturing Promotion (SOFOFA) has become an active promoter of social engagement on the part of its members.[52]

Also important in the diffusion process have been the Latin press and Latin universities. La Nación in Argentina publishes a monthly "Solidarity Community" edition. The Argentine business magazines, *Negocios* and *Mercado,* do regular rankings of corporations in terms of their social responsibility performance. The press was especially helpful to the diffusion of the social responsibility ethic in Brazil. As noted already, Instituto Ethos made active and effective use of the media to advance its mission, and key reporters, many of them refugees from the same 1968 college protests against the military regime as the progressive business leaders, were only too happy to help. Universities such as Universidad de San Andres in Argentina and Universidad de los Andes in Colombia have organized training courses and research programs focused squarely on CSR. Chile boasts six degree programs in CSR.

Another key source of CSR promotion was the multinational firms that entered the Latin American region so prominently in the 1990s. Many of these firms had highly developed CSR programs in their parent companies that were exported to Latin America and adapted to local circumstances. The Look Good . . . Feel Better campaign launched by the Argentine cosmetics industry was thus modeled on a U.S. Cosmetics Industry Foundation program. Impulsar Foundation, aimed at promoting youth entrepreneurship, was similarly modeled on a UK Youth Business International program and brought to Argentina by a former employee of a UK mining company. As a general rule, the multinationals were less likely than the homegrown firms to buy into the discourse of citizen participation that makes the Latin American version of corporate social engagement so distinctive, but they certainly helped propagate the standard MBA approach to the topic.

Finally, and by no means incidentally, was the push given to corporate social engagement in the region by a number of outside private foundations and international organizations. One of these was the Kellogg Foundation under the leadership of regional director Marcos Kisil. Kisil, himself a participant in the early PNBE developments, occupied a strategic position in the development of the corporate social engagement phenomenon in Brazil and elsewhere in the region. Kellogg thus provided some of the earliest support to the ABRINQ Foundation, underwrote the initial development of GIFE, funded the trip that introduced Oded Grajew to Business for Social Responsibility and led to the creation of Instituto Ethos, and then provided funding for the early start-up of this institute.[53]

Another key player in the emergence of corporate social engagement in Latin America was the Inter-American Foundation, the unusual agency of the U.S. government set up to pursue an alternative approach to development in Latin America focusing on the promotion of grass-roots organizations. IAF has played a particularly important role in promoting the participatory and partnering themes in both the discourse and practice of Latin American corporate social engagement. As IAF explains in its materials: "Unlike other U.S. Government foreign assistance agencies, the IAF neither channels its resources through governments, nor designs programs or projects for implementation in the region. Instead, it focuses on small-scale local projects that address the needs of poor people in a manner that enhances self-reliance."[54]

In a sense, IAF stumbled into partnerships with businesses in the region beginning in the early 1990s when it was approached by officials from PDVSA, Venezuela's state-owned oil company, with a request for help in connecting to the indigenous communities in which the company was conducting its exploration and drilling activities. The result was the creation of a joint fund supported by both PDVSA and IAF to fund grass-roots development projects involving local organizations and leaders.[55] The success of this effort gave rise to the concept of mobilizing the Latin American business community in support of grass-roots development activities and the grass-roots organizations that IAF had been supporting in the region for two decades. IAF offices in the Andean region were particularly active in promoting this idea, and IAF emerged as a significant supporter of the embryonic corporate social engagement initiatives in the region, focusing particularly on the early diffusion of a highly participatory style of social engagement activity. Thus, IAF provided early support to GIFE and ABRINQ in Brazil and followed this up with a series of additional grants to Instituto Ethos and some of the early corporate foundations. In Colombia, IAF was a major supporter of the Colombia Center on Philanthropy created in partnership with Fundación Social. And IAF support was critical to virtually every one of the CEMEFI corporate social engagement initiatives in Mexico.[56] Indeed, one observer went so far as to credit IAF with being "the parent of CSR in Latin America."[57]

Most recently, IAF has organized a network of corporate foundations willing to support a grass-roots style of development work, featuring extensive grass-roots participation and corporate partnerships with the grass-roots civil society organizations that manage it. As will be detailed more fully in Chapter 4 below, the resulting RedEAmerica network is both a "learning network" among some 60 corporate foundations and a joint funding mechanism, channeling corporate support into projects that feature grass-roots approaches to development.[58]

Also important have been the annual CSR conferences organized by the Inter-American Development Bank. These have usefully put the imprimatur of a major regional institution on the CSR concept, provided a sizable gathering spot and visibility for CSR professionals, and yielded a rich harvest of CSR materials.

Conclusion

In short, a substantial movement is afoot in Latin America to engage the corporate sector in social and environmental problem solving. This movement has been driven in important part by significant political, economic, and social changes that have weakened traditional social protections, increased social tensions, changed the structure of the region's enterprises, and exposed corporations to new citizen demands. While many businesses have remained mired in traditional conceptions of their social responsibilities, newer elements of the business community, including many operating far from their home bases, have responded to these pressures by embracing a progressive concept of the role of business in society, a concept that views businesses as key social, not just economic, actors, with a responsibility to take an active role in addressing societal problems. What is more, the corporate social engagement discourse in Latin America has acquired its own distinct tones, stressing the moral and not just the economic bases for corporate involvement, acknowledging a more explicit need to involve communities, and recognizing that corporate social engagement must involve not only the external operations of corporations but also their internal ones. As one longtime participant in the movement put it: "In contemporary times, a company has two contracts: an 'economic contract' with its investors and a 'social contract' with the community to improve the quality of life and the environment."[59]

Not only are businesses pursuing these activities individually, but they also are joining forces through promotional bodies that seek to elevate the visibility of these business initiatives, to persuade other businesses to join in, and thus to help change longstanding negative public attitudes toward business. These diffusion efforts have been encouraged, moreover, by a number of outside organizations that see in them an opportunity to expand the pool of resources, talents, and contacts that can be mustered to help solve the region's social and economic problems.

To be sure, this entire process remains embryonic in many places and far from uniform even where it is most developed. As one observer in Chile noted, "We still have much work to do to put the [CSR] idea into the blood of the people."[60] At this point, the rhetoric of CSR has far surpassed the reality, creating a condition that one set of analysts has called "terminology inflation."[61] Yet there seems enough momentum behind the movement to suggest that it is here to stay, and enough notable achievements to hope that it does. It is to an assessment of these achievements that we must therefore now turn.

Chapter 3

Professionalization

Nothing is possible without men; nothing is lasting without institutions.

—Jean Monnet, 1978[1]

Argentina's Banco Galicia is a venerable institution with a one-hundred-year history of service to its customers and a long tradition of charitable support for its employees and the communities in which they live. But Argentina's 2001 economic crisis produced a "crisis within a crisis" for the bank as its depositors fled to the safety of larger multinational institutions. To woo them back, the bank turned to an unusual quarter: the volunteer helping activities that its employees undertook to assist families hurt by the economic downturn. Inspired by these activities and the positive impact they were having on the bank's customers, the bank formulated a new business strategy around the theme of helping the communities it serves to grow and replaced its longstanding personal style of philanthropy with a more coherent social engagement strategy to reinforce it. New institutional arrangements, a focused set of activities, and mechanisms for continued employee involvement were all part of the resulting package. By 2006 the bank had adopted a new mission statement, a mandatory code of ethics for its two thousand suppliers, new loan risk criteria that included environmental requirements, and a restructured grant program focused more tightly on three areas and managed by a new employee-controlled institution, the Associación Civil Ayudando a Ayudar (The Helping to Help Association).[2]

This evolution of Banco Galicia's community engagement activities from personalized charity to professionalized corporate social engagement is being repeated in board rooms throughout the Latin American region, with varying conviction and speed but a striking degree of commonality. Inspiring this process have been two important impulses: first, the growing conviction promoted by the diffusion agents that, in the context of Latin America, business social engagement is essential not just for business success but for business *survival*, given the hostile business environment that exists; and second, the conviction advanced by the "MBA mindset" mentioned earlier that business philanthropy, like other aspects of business operations, needs not only to be expanded but also to be transformed from the personal benefaction of business owners and their families into a professionalized component of business operations that is approached with the same discipline, professionalism, and strategic focus as any other.

While there are many different ideas about how this should be done, there seems to be widespread agreement that it involves at least three important elements: first, *institutionalizing* the function so that it is less sporadic and more regular; second, *reconceptualizing* the activity so that it is less diffuse and more strategic; and third, *integrating* the activity more fully into the life of the business.[3]

This chapter examines how far Latin American businesses have moved down the road to meeting this professionalization challenge. To be sure, as noted in Chapter 1, this is not the only dimension in terms of which the evolution of corporate social engagement in the region should be assessed. But it provides a useful backdrop for consideration of the others by portraying the basic "machinery"—the institutions, personnel, and ideas—that Latin American corporations are increasingly bringing to their social engagement activities.

Institutionalization:
From Ad Hoc to Sustained Engagement

One of the major complaints about the traditional approach to business philanthropy in Latin America has been that its ad hoc and sporadic character made it difficult to access and impossible to rely on. As one set of observers put it: "Companies projected themselves as families in which workers were cast as children and employers as their protectors."[4] Assistance therefore depended almost entirely on the whims and predilections of the leading families.

A central thrust of the new corporate social engagement paradigm has been to regularize corporate social engagement and make it more transparent and open, to take philanthropy out of the back pocket of the owner and vest it in an identifiable institutional structure staffed by skilled professionals knowledgeable about the problems they are addressing.

One manifestation of this thrust has been the emergence of corporate foundations or institutes in companies throughout the region. This development began as early as the 1960s in some countries, such as Colombia, but accelerated in the 1980s. By 1997, Colombia had ninety-four corporate foundations with assets of almost US$1billion.[5] Most of the foundations in Latin America, in fact, are corporate foundations. They represent an institutional manifestation of the desire to get beyond the personalistic, paternalistic style of corporate philanthropy characteristic of the region's past, with its close links to the clientilism that has characterized the region's politics. Indeed, GIFE was explicitly created to break this link between paternalistic philanthropy and clientilistic politics and promote a more progressive image of modern philanthropic action. GIFE took shape against the background of the campaign to impeach President Collor de Mello, the first democratically elected president after the ouster of Brazil's military regime. Because Collor's crime was diverting funds raised by a charitable organization for personal gain, the founders of GIFE wanted to make the point that charitable institutions could be run in a professional and transparent way.[6]

By no means have all of Latin America's businesses, or even its "leading" businesses, embraced the foundation as the best institutional vehicle for effective corporate social engagement, however. Indeed, the early enthusiasm for separate corporate foundations may already have peaked in the region. A study of corporate philanthropy programs in Argentina, for example, revealed that even among the larger corporations, only 20 percent had established corporate foundations as of the mid 1990s, and most of these were companies that were parts of multinational corporations. A decade later that figure still stood at only 25 percent.[7] Even where foundations exist, their functions have often been highly constrained. Few corporate foundations have true endowments, and most are overseen by the chief executive officer of the company or by vice presidents for community relations or marketing. Although there has been substantial upgrading of the tools and techniques for guiding foundations and corporations in their social engagement functions, as of 2005 only about half of Argentina's corporate foundations had documented policies identifying their targeted areas of interest and only 16 percent had published guidelines and application procedures.[8] Similar findings are evident from research in Brazil. There, the number of corporations that have institutionalized their philanthropic giving by creating corporate foundations or similar entities remains small. GIFE, the association of the more highly structured of these institutions, numbers only 100 members, and 10 percent of these are companies rather than company foundations. Key decisions on business social engagement remain in the hands of owners or shareholders rather than professional staff, and corporate philanthropy responsibilities in many companies often sit side by side with public relations and public affairs, frequently in the same person. As one Brazilian corporate philanthropy official put it: "Eighty percent of my time I do corporate public affairs and 20 percent I do corporate philanthropy."

One reason for this apparent slowing in the formation of corporate foundations may be a growing reluctance of corporate leaders to surrender control to a quasi-independent unit. Indeed, some corporate foundations have found their wings clipped by corporate managers eager to tie corporate actions more closely to company objectives. This seems to have been the case, for example, with Minera Escondida, the Chilean copper company, which recently restructured its giving programs to reduce the independence of its formerly relatively autonomous foundation. While this is in line with the MBA approach discussed earlier, it has produced a degree of resentment on the ground by reducing community input into corporate objectives.

Also at work, however, has been an intriguing pattern of experimentation with alternative institutional mechanisms through which Latin American companies have begun to pursue their corporate social engagement functions. Illustrative is the evolution of the social engagement machinery of the Corona Corporation in Colombia, a major manufacturer of household fixtures.[9]

Like many Latin American companies, Corona has a long history of philanthropic involvement. But the early forms were handled informally in classic Latin *patron* fashion. In the 1960s, however, the company began to formalize its philanthropy, creating the Fundación St. Helena. The choice of name was revealing, emphasizing the religious roots of the company's social engagement but also the company's reluctance to associate its own name too closely with the activities for fear that this might suggest that the company was undertaking them for commercial rather than moral reasons. By the 1980s these qualms had diminished, and the company's ambitions for its social engagement function expanded, requiring another institutional shift. Fundación St. Helena was renamed Fundación Corona, its purely philanthropic and charitable activities in the vicinity of the company's plants returned to the individual plants to manage, and the new foundation unleashed to focus on broader societal problem solving. Then, in the 1990s, the company set out on a new wave of institutional innovation including establishing a set of quasi-corporate/quasi-nonprofit entities to pursue various social objectives: Corporación Calidad to promote quality, Centro de Gestión Hospital to promote improved health care, and Prodencia to execute education projects. This reflected another interesting trend in Latin American corporate social activities—a tendency to create new entities directly overseen by the corporation rather than relying on existing nonprofit organizations, a point to which we will return in the discussion of the partnership theme in Chapter 4. Finally, in 2002, Fundación Corona fostered the creation of yet another organization, Empresarios por la Educación, this time a coalition of more than one hundred corporations that have come together to pursue a long-term agenda of educational improvement.

This penchant of Latin corporations to establish new institutional structures to handle their community engagement activities is hardly peculiar to Colombia or to the Corona Corporation. For example, the Bimbo Group in Mexico, a major producer of bread and other food products, moved as early as 1963 to help create the Mexican Foundation for Rural Development.[10] And the Paschoal Group in Brazil established Fundação Educar in the early 1990s to introduce new approaches into the Brazilian educational system. Here, again, the company shied away from using its own name for the entity in line with the prevailing "Do it, but don't show it" philosophy of corporate philanthropy.[11]

Equally interesting is the institutional structure that has evolved in one of Mexico's most significant banks, Banamex, now a part of Citigroup.[12] Banamex established two foundations—Fomento Social Banamex and Fomento Ecologia Banamex—in the 1990s, but the foundations really function as holding companies for a set of separate "trust funds" within the bank. Through the trust-fund structure Banamex can assemble resources from multiple donors, including government, and bring them to bear on priority projects. Currently, fifty such trust funds are in operation, with assets of US$100 million. One such fund supports a loan program for peasants; it began during an economic crisis twelve years earlier and has now evolved, with the addition of Inter-American Development Bank funding, into the country's most important source of small agricultural loans and a vehicle through which to wean farmers in the guerrilla areas away from drug production and into organic coffee. Another fund is seeking to convert old haciendas into hotels. A third is supporting the construction of low-income housing in cooperation with Habitat for Humanity, and a fourth is providing assistance for disaster relief in the wake of natural disasters. These funds provide focused mechanisms for bringing the financial acumen of the bank together with a variety of resources to address pressing societal problems without having to create entirely new institutions.

This institutional experimentation reveals both the seriousness and the creativity with which at least some Latin American companies have been pursuing their corporate social engagement activities and their considerable reluctance to rely on either government or the nonprofit sector to advance their social engagement goals. The companies believe they can do this job better themselves, that they have the answers and the technical capacity not only to decide what is needed but to get it done. They have thus moved beyond creating foundations through which to distribute support to others and begun creating their own operating entities to carry out projects and programs directly.

Side by side with the institutionalization of social engagement in the region has been the growth of dedicated corporate engagement staff. Research in Argentina found that, at least among the leading corporations, 57 percent of the companies and 76 percent of the foundations had staff specifically assigned to manage business social engagement activities in 2005, even though the staff sometimes had other functions as well. This was up from 32 percent of the corporations and 52 percent of the foundations in 1997.[13] Similar growth of professional staff has also been documented in Brazil, where the larger companies were reported to employ an average of five staff members in their social engagement operations.[14] Some corporate social engagement staffs have expanded well beyond this, of course. Mexico's Fundación Televisa, for example, employs twenty-five people.[15] Banamex employs ten staff members in its two major foundations.[16]

This growth in staff has, in turn, triggered an expansion of training opportunities—seminars, conferences, university courses, and even university degree programs. All of this has helped to breathe a spirit of excitement into the field despite the frustrations that operating within a corporate administrative structure sometimes entails. Increasingly, companies are coming to view these social engagement specialists as sources of social intelligence for the corporation on how to deal with communities. To take advantage of this, some corporations have pulled their foundations and foundation officers back into the firms. This has happened with the cosmetics firm Boticário and the Brazilian Gerdau steel company, for example, while other companies, such as Brazil's ABN AMRO Bank, have skipped the foundation phase altogether and established "sustainability officers" within their corporations to manage a broad set of activities geared to sustaining the corporation over the long run by attending to its external environment in all its facets.[17] Whether this represents a progressive development that integrates the social engagement function more firmly into the fabric of the business or a retrogressive one that limits the independence and discretion of corporate social engagement professionals depends on the depth of commitment to this mission on the part of key corporate managers. In the cases cited here, that commitment appears strong.

Strategic Corporate Philanthropy: The Search for Focus

In addition to institutionalizing corporate social engagement, the drive toward professionalization has also involved a search for greater focus and an effort, as we have seen, to integrate social engagement with broader corporate business strategies.[18] This line of thinking has had special resonance in Latin America, where traditional business philanthropy has long been faulted for being "scattered and limited in its impact."[19] But it has also taken its own Latin "flavor," reflecting the special social circumstances that have helped to propel the corporate social engagement impulse in the region.

Fernando Rossetti, the executive director of GIFE in Brazil, thus sees five phases of corporate foundation development in Brazil.[20] As reflected in Figure 3–1, in the first phase companies handle their philanthropic activities directly in an ad hoc, personal manner and rely on a charity or *assistentialist* concept dealing with symptoms, not causes. In Phase II the philanthropic function is institutionalized, often in a corporate foundation, and an accretion of diverse projects occurs, though with little clear focus or strategic ties to the company. In Phase III the foundation enters a "focus crisis" and begins a search for direction. Phase IV is the strategic phase in which the foundation develops a clearer mission and formulates programs in line with it. In Phase V the foundation realizes that its programs alone cannot make effective progress against the issues it is addressing, that collaboration is needed, including with government, and that the foundation must therefore help to stimulate the political activism that will help promote the needed policy changes.

Figure 3–1. Phases of Foundation Development

By Rossetti's estimate, even in Brazil, perhaps the leading CSR country in the region, and even among the members of GIFE, which represents the foundations with the most substantial and advanced CSR programs, only about 40 percent have advanced to Phase IV, while an additional 5 percent are in Phase III. Research by Brazil's IPEA seems to confirm this: although 57 percent of companies claimed in a 2004 survey that their social investments were aligned with a corporate strategy or plan, only 6 percent could report that the strategy was enshrined in any kind of formal document.[21] Elsewhere, the progress along this continuum is even less fully advanced. An analysis of corporate social engagement in Chile, for example, reports that this activity is utilized basically as a marketing device. "The correct CSE language is being applied, but in most cases its use is only conceptual while actual applications are superficial."[22] In Argentina, as well, the vast majority of corporations and foundations still adhere to a traditional philanthropic approach. Even in Brazil, critics complain about the public relations character of much corporate social engagement, citing data showing that a full third of the limited sums available for corporate philanthropy goes into materials publicizing the activity.[23]

At the same time, there are notable signs of progress everywhere, many of them consistent with the advanced thinking in the field stressing the need to link corporate social engagement to what Porter and Kramer term "the competitive context" of businesses, that is, the features of the environment that determine whether the company will have the factors of production, the demand for its products, the legal environment, and the supportive industries to operate effectively.[24] In the context of Latin America this has meant a heavy emphasis on education. This reflects the fact that the lack of sufficient numbers of educated workers acts as a significant brake on competitiveness in the region, though the fact that education is a "safe" arena for corporate involvement may also be at work. Thus, for example, research in Brazil indicates that education is the dominant area of social engagement for 64 percent of the corporations surveyed, and the same is true in Argentina and Chile.[25]

In a number of cases corporations have tied their support for education more closely to their corporate missions. Thus, in

Argentina, Fundación YPF, an outgrowth of the privatization of Argentina's former state-owned petroleum company, has focused its efforts on improving science education, with a particular emphasis on graduate and postgraduate education in the field of energy, clearly important for the company's business.[26] Similarly, Microsoft Colombia's corporate social engagement mission is to "tap the talents of employees to promote digital inclusion and education to unleash people's potential," a goal firmly anchored to Microsoft's core business. In pursuit of this goal Microsoft has organized thirty-two Community Technology Centers to train local people in the use of computers, using, of course, Microsoft Office as the training material.[27]

As we have suggested, however, in the context of Latin America, where a deep chasm still divides the population at large from the business elite and where a sense of impending crisis pervades the business environment, this close tie between corporate social engagement and corporate business needs has real limits. In the face of serious popular suspicions, corporations have felt obliged to go well beyond the concept of "competitive environment," or at least to stretch that concept well beyond its typical North American meaning, to embrace social engagement activities only marginally related to direct business functions but necessary to maintain the corporation's "license to operate" in the Latin American environment. Thus, for example, Fundación YPF in Argentina found it propitious in the midst of the Argentine fiscal crisis of 2001 to supplement its targeted program of postgraduate energy education with a social development program aimed at community needs in the vicinity of its facilities. Microsoft Colombia similarly operates a series of "social projects" in addition to its digital inclusion efforts, and not alone for public-relations purposes. It feels obliged to sensitize its employees to their social responsibilities as part of a conscious effort to make sure Microsoft workers do not become alienated from the society in which they operate.[28]

In a number of cases, moreover, corporations have developed more sophisticated approaches to social programming. One of the most impressive and well-known of these was the largely successful effort by Brazil's ABN AMRO Bank under the direction of CEO Fabio Barossa to re-brand the institution following a major merger as "a new bank for a new society," a "bank of value" delivering benefits not only to its stockholders and customers, but to society as well. Central to this re-branding was a coherent corporate social engagement strategy that tapped the financial expertise of the bank to create a micro-credit program for small-scale enterprises, established new lending criteria incorporating environmental considerations, and took a number of other measures to affect how the bank does business (as detailed more fully in Chapter 6 below).[29]

Alpina, a producer of milk and milk products in Colombia, has gone through a similar process of broad re-conceptualization of the company's relation to society. In Alpina's case, the rethinking was triggered by concerns in the company's human resources department about the impact of Colombia's 2002 economic crisis on the morale both of the country and of the company's employees. To address this concern, the department launched a campaign emphasizing the theme that everyone could do something to improve the country. To illustrate this, the department called on employees to identify the ways in which, as Alpina employees, they were already helping their country, focusing on the company's function as a "good employer," its attention to quality and nutrition in its products, its community work in the area of nutrition education, and its contribution to the society in the form of paying taxes and abiding by the law. This was the first time that a full register of Alpina's social engagement actions had been assembled, and the results significantly enhanced worker self-image and sense of mission. Against this backdrop human relations department staff then launched an elaborate effort to forge a forward-looking corporate social engagement strategy that assessed what each of the company's stakeholders could expect to get out of the company's social engagement activities, what lines of action this would entail, and what level of effort this would require. Under the slogan "Alpina is all of us," the result was an unusually comprehensive linkage of corporate social engagement activities to corporate stakeholders and a strategy for utilizing social engagement to reenergize employees and reengage stakeholders.[30]

Yet another approach is evident in the work of the Avina Foundation of Colombia. A newcomer to the corporate foundation world in Colombia, but not in Latin America generally, Avina set about conceptualizing its focus even before starting up its operations. In particular, the foundation launched a year-long planning process to "recognize the country through Avina's lens."

Through conversations with some 350 people, it formulated a "map of opportunities," identifying three areas of action around a central theme of "a country working toward reconciliation and peacemaking." As the Avina Foundation director for Colombia put it, Avina "doesn't like to think of itself as a funder but as an actor in society." The idea, clearly, is to bridge the chasm that separates the corporate sector from the rest of society. Reflecting this, of the three areas of action identified, only one—a focus on water—is directly related to a business that is a source of the foundation's funds. The other two—strengthening democracy and generating wealth with equality—go well beyond narrow corporate concerns, though they have a potentially enormous long-term impact on the ability of this and other companies to function in this violence-torn country.[31]

Backward Linkage: Engaging Employees

Another facet of the professionalization and maturation of corporate social engagement in Latin America has been an increased effort to diffuse corporate social engagement within the corporations. This, too, reflects an effort to get beyond the traditional, family-dominated mode of philanthropic activity that has long been characteristic of the region by moving corporate social engagement out of the front office and into the back offices as well. One rationale for such moves is to solidify the position of corporate social engagement within the company. The managers of Fundação Telefônica in Brazil, for example, launched an employee volunteering program precisely to overcome a pervasive isolation of the foundation from the rest of the company and to integrate it more fully into the life of the corporation.[32] But as the Alpina example showed, such employee engagement can also serve other corporate objectives, such as boosting employee morale and attaching employees more firmly to the company, thus reducing the turnover of scarce technical talent. What is more, as illustrated in the case of Argentina's Banco Galicia mentioned earlier, employee volunteering can also help attract customers and thereby affect the bottom line more directly.

To be sure, in this dimension of professionalization, as in most others, there are enormous disparities within the region and even within particular countries. In its study of corporate philanthropy in Brazil, for example, IPEA found that only 31 percent of Brazilian corporations engaged their employees in their social actions, though among the larger companies this reached 75 percent. Research in Argentina similarly found limited scope for employee involvement in corporate social engagement, with only 30 percent of the companies offering matching gift arrangements.[33]

Nevertheless, a number of intriguing examples of employee involvement are also visible. One manifestation of this is the growth of formal corporate volunteering programs. One study in Argentina, for example, reported that all the leading corporations have organized such programs (see Table 3–1), and the growth of organized employee volunteering is evident elsewhere as well.[34] Beyond this, other imaginative techniques of employee engagement have surfaced. As noted earlier, for example, Banco Galicia in Argentina has taken the bold step of outsourcing a significant part of its contributions program to a separate civil society organization, Associación Civil Ayudando a Ayudar (the Civil Association Helping to Help), essentially run by a committee of employees. The YPF Foundation gives employees the right to propose community projects for funding from the foundation, and over three hundred such proposals were submitted in a recent year. Every such project must have two employee promoters and at least one civil society organization partner.[35] The Alpina strategy development process described earlier similarly utilized a bottom-up approach to identify its targets in order to make this not the "company's program" but the employees' program. ABN AMRO has created a Children's Fund that has managed to engage nearly half of the bank's employees, and has trained employees to evaluate projects and not just distribute grants.[36] Microsoft Colombia has gone beyond this by creating a system of committees—involving both company employees and their families—to manage each program in the company's social engagement portfolio. A family member serves as the "lead" on each of these committees, and a Microsoft employee serves as the operational head. Thanks to this structure Microsoft Solidaria, the company's foundation, can operate six different programs with just two staff members. As the regional director of Microsoft explained: "Employees love this. It connects them and their families to Microsoft and its mission."[37]

Table 3–1. Illustrative Examples of Corporate Volunteering Programs: Argentina

Volunteer Programs	Characteristics
BankBoston	In 1996 the bank's institutional relations area—with the support of its corporate foundation—established a corporate volunteering program called Águilas Solidarias. The program focuses on children and youth, and its preliminary initiatives were the organization of puppet shows in public hospitals and promoting recycling activities. Between 1998 and 2003, one thousand employees dedicated 6,330 hours to these activities.
American Express	Seventy percent of American Express's employees in Argentina participate in the company's volunteer program. This program is a local embodiment of American Express's Global Volunteer Action Fund, which channels resources to employees volunteering in non-profit organizations around the world.
Fundación Telefónica	Fundación Telefónica not only runs a volunteer program but trains employees to serve in it. Over 650 employees now participate in the program.
Fundación C&A	C&A, a department-store chain, runs a corporate volunteer program focused on education, especially early childhood education. Twenty-five percent of C&A employees working in Argentina participate in this program. The program operates under a council made up of managers and supervisors who analyze the initiatives to be supported, facilitate employees' participation, and ensure that the program fits within the mission.
TNT Argentina	TNT Argentina runs a volunteer program called Ida y Vuelta, which allows employees to commit five working days each month to work with students at a nearby school. The company also adds pediatric support every other week between March and December. Food, clothes, and medicine collections are also organized by the program.

Source: Based on Gabriel Berger, *The New Alliance for Progress: Patterns of Business Engagement in Latin America—The Case of Argentina* (2007).

More generally, corporate foundations, and the growing number of corporate social engagement staff within companies, have taken on the role of *provocateurs* within companies, provoking companies to pay attention to social engagement and providing vehicles through which to do so.[38] Their biggest impact, therefore, may come less through the budgets they command, which are typically quite small, than through the changes they can induce in corporate behavior more geneally, a topic to which we will return in a subsequent chapter.

Conclusion

In short, an interesting process of maturation and professionalization is under way in the field of corporate social engagement in Latin America. Corporations are institutionalizing corporate social engagement, formulating more coherent corporate social engagement strategies, tying these strategies to broader corporate objectives, and engaging larger numbers of company employees in the efforts.

As with so much in this field, developments are uneven, and there is much "to-ing" and "fro-ing" even within individual firms, suggesting the uncertainty that exists about some of the central concepts and how they should be applied. As one recent illustration of this, Alpina's human relations department no sooner put the finishing touches on its elaborate corporate social engagement matrix, with its carefully constructed menu of activities and estimates of their probable payoffs to a variety of corporate stakeholders, than new leadership entered the picture. This new leadership had a much more narrow conception of how the corporation should relate to its stakeholders and dismissed the entire game plan and replaced the principal architects.

Nevertheless, the sense of development and excitement in this field is palpable. Not only are Latin American corporations increasingly adopting modes of corporate social engagement consistent with best practices being promoted from afar, but also they are adapting these best practices to local circumstances in often imaginative and creative ways and generating their own important innovations.

Chapter 4

Partnering

Establishing connections with enterprises is difficult; it is a day by day effort.
—Juan Pedro Pinochet, Un Techo para Chile[1]

It was three years ago, when he was nine years old, that Paco noticed his school routine had changed considerably. He did not know why, but his school class was split into three parts. He found himself suddenly confronted with an unusual situation: one teacher with only fifteen pupils. They were more or less the same age and he felt recognized by his tutor for the first time. Don Franco, his math teacher, told the children that a well-meaning corporate foundation had chosen their school for a pilot project. Paco experienced the difference from the first day. The teachers seemed more interested and they had time for individual questions. Paco felt a new self-confidence in regard to his studies. His marks improved, because his teachers improved their lessons with creative group work. They also got computers and computer lessons, which Paco particularly enjoyed. Don Franco told them that this project would not be finished after a year, as was usually the case with the government projects. The foundation signed a contract with the school for fifteen years. Best of all, Don Franco told Paco that if he continued to do well with his computer classes, he had a good chance to go on to college to study computer science; the foundation was offering scholarships for good students like him, something no one in his family had ever dreamed of.

Paco's good fortune was the byproduct of an extraordinary partnership forged by a group of Colombian corporations in 2002 to promote long-term improvements in Colombia's grossly underfunded and patchy educational system. The partnership now boasts more than one hundred member corporations joined together through a new institution, Empresarios por la Educación (ExE) (Businesses for Education). ExE styles itself a "second floor organization." Rather than operating programs itself, it stimulates the formation of local business coalitions to promote educational improvement in their respective regions and provides technical and financial assistance to match local resources. In addition to broadening public awareness of the importance of education and mobilizing business involvement in school management, ExE has launched a school-improvement program— Modelos Escolares para la Equidad (Model Schools for Equity—MEPE)—that is designed to improve pedagogical techniques while also addressing the broader social context needed to connect schools to their communities in a positive way. The MEPE project in Paco's hometown of Manizales is one of the most advanced examples of what ExE hopes to accomplish in dozens of communities throughout the country.[2]

The formation of ExE underscores a fundamental reality about corporate social engagement in Latin America, and many other places as well: few corporations acting on their own can get real traction on the kind of social and economic problems that confront their societies. To go beyond symbolic public-relations efforts and make meaningful inroads on significant societal problems, corporations must join forces with other corporations, and with other social actors—in government and civil society.

While the rationale for cooperation is compelling, the obstacles are significant. As James Austin and others have warned, forging and managing partnerships is not a task for the faint of heart. It requires perseverance, a tolerance for ambiguity, and an ability to absorb disappointments. This is particularly the case when it comes to cross-sector partnerships involving not only different institutions, but also different *kinds* of institutions. Almost inevitably, such partnerships run into institutional imbalances and differences in culture, making it difficult to find a common language, to align time perspectives, and to overcome misleading stereotypes.[3]

The Record to Date

The Latin American record of business involvement in cross-sectoral partnerships to pursue social engagement activities displays all of these dynamics, and more. By some measures, the collaboration record in the region is quite impressive, especially given the relative novelty of the region's corporate social responsibility movement. Research in Argentina, for example, demonstrates that by 2004, civil society organizations had become a major, if not *the* major, destination of corporate donations, with 93 percent of surveyed companies reporting such donations.[4]

Elsewhere as well there is heartening evidence of corporate involvement with civil society. IPEA's research in Brazil, for example, reveals that nonprofit organizations are the most common partners of corporations there as well, with 57 percent of surveyed companies reporting such partnerships. In Chile, one estimate puts the share of medium and large enterprises engaged in some kind of relationship with an NGO at 50 percent.[5]

In addition to the cooperation between corporations and civil society there is significant evidence of a growing pattern of cooperation *among* corporations and corporate foundations. Kramer and Porter have argued that social engagement may be one area where the normal competitive pressures of the market leave ample room for cooperation in order to address problems in the environment that are impeding the business community as a whole.[6] Perhaps reflecting this, a recent study in Argentina revealed that 53 percent of 152 firms reporting involvement in social initiatives as of 2004 were involved in initiatives financed by multiple sponsors.[7] While not all of these were jointly managed undertakings, at least some were (see Box 4–2).

Elsewhere in the region as well there is evidence of corporate cooperation in undertaking social initiatives. A study by GIFE in Brazil similarly found that 83 percent of its members reported working in partnership with other institutions. A broader survey of corporate social engagement in Brazil revealed that 27 percent of companies claimed to be involved in joint initiatives with other companies.[8] Some of these, such as the Todos pela Educacion initiative organized by a number of major corporations with the goal

Box 4–1. Corporate-Nonprofit Partnership: *Diario La Nación* and Red Solidaria

La Nación is one of Argentina's oldest newspapers, having begun publication in 1870. Historically, the paper has also been widely known for its social commitment, both to its personnel and the community in general. One mode of community involvement consisted of publishing news concerning welfare activities of several social organizations (for example, Patronato de la Infancia (Infants' Home), Argentine Red Cross, and the Salvation Army).

However, in the mid 1990s *La Nación* faced a change in its management that led to new momentum in its corporate social actions. In 1999 La Nación Newspaper Foundation was established, systematizing and turning the company's social initiatives into an explicit policy. As one of its initiatives, the newspaper launched a monthly special section called "Solidarity."

Around this time the paper was approached by social entrepreneur Juan Carr, who had founded a unique volunteer-based social institution called Red Solidaria (RS) through which citizens in need of help could locate people or institutions able to lend a hand. Over a period of six years, RS built up a network of twenty-eight regular volunteers who manned the telephone lines from their homes and helped more than 220,000 people (HIV patients, cancer patients, children suffering from malnutrition, people affected by floods, and more).

Faced with a request from a young man who needed a delicate operation (available only in the United States) but lacked the money to pay for it, Carr approached *La Nación* for help. The result was a joint appeal carried through the pages of the newspaper that not only awakened a powerful response in the population but also had an enormous impact on the newspaper and its employees. Shortly thereafter, Red Solidaria and *La Nación* entered into a joint venture called the "Solidarity Classifieds," a daily feature in the newspaper that offers free ads for nonprofits looking for in-kind donations and volunteers, as well as for people willing to volunteer and looking for nonprofits through which to do so. The section has been included in the last page of the "Want Ads" published daily and has become the centerpiece of the paper's social engagement activities, involving a wide range of the paper's staff.

Box 4-2. Philanthropic Collaboration among Corporations, Argentina

Corporations	Program/Project
Arcor Antorchas	Aimed at the well-being of children and youngsters in Córdoba.
Antorchas Burge and Born Navarro Viola	Aimed at schools in Chaco.
Arcor Minetti	Since 2002, the program has aimed at upgrading educational opportunities of thirteen thousand boys and girls localted in Córdoba.
YPF Bunge and Born	Upgraded the study of sciences through an environmental project.
Antorchas Bunge and Born Navarro Viola	Granted scholarships to outstanding students.
YPF Bunge and Born	Supported CSOs that provided Internet access to libraries located in the Patagonia region, offering additional Internet training.
Arcor Acindar Navarro Viola	Educational Opportunities at the Community Level program. This program supports initiatives stemming from local CSOs' collaboration processes targeted at improving education in highly vulnerable communities located in different provinces.
Minetti Telefonic Bank Boston	Early Education program. This program offers support to CSO-driven projects aimed at improving preschool education levels in highly vulnerable communities.

Sources: M. Paladino and A. Mohan. *Tendencias de Responsabilidad Social en Argentina,* Documento de Investigación (Buenos Aires: IAE/Universidad Austral, Aces, Pilar, 2002), cited in Berger, *The New Alliance for Progress: Patterns of Business Engagement in Latin America—The Case of Argentina,* unpublished report (2007).

of promoting five strategic changes in the Brazilian educational system by 2022, the 200th anniversary of Brazilian Independence, are major undertakings with long-term goals and potentially sustained funding.

Beyond the formal collaborations, moreover, there is considerable informal interaction among corporate social responsibility staff. The number of corporate social responsibility seminars, award programs, classes, conferences, and informal get-togethers has mushroomed in the region. CSR personnel, at least among the larger companies, now form a close-knit network both within countries and among them. What is more, there is a palpable excitement in the field and a certain spirit of adventure as new ideas are tried and new trends established. All of this creates a climate in which partnerships and joint action become increasingly feasible.

While there is solid evidence of collaboration in the Latin American corporate social engagement environment, however, considerable caution must be shown in interpreting this evidence. For one thing, many of the jointly sponsored undertakings are not true collaborations but just projects that multiple corporations happen to finance. In addition, in the case of corporate-nonprofit links, the share of corporate resources flowing to nonprofit organizations is far smaller than the numbers of engagements might suggest. One study of the larger corporations and foundations in Argentina, for example, found that while initiatives involving nonprofit organizations represented 46 percent of the initiatives funded by these foundations, they accounted for only 25 percent of the funds these organizations allocated for social purposes.[9] A similar story emerges from a study of corporate foundation behavior in Brazil. According to this survey, Brazilian corporate foundations devote one-third of their budgets to direct projects run by the foundations or their institutes and one-third to public-relations materials, leaving at most one-third for direct support to NGOs.[10]

These findings seem to be confirmed by the detailed assessment of corporate-civil society partnerships in Latin America undertaken by James Austin and his colleagues through the Social Enterprise Knowledge Network. Austin and his collaborators were able to identify only a handful of truly integrative partnerships among the twenty-four model corporate-nonprofit partnerships that they identified and examined in depth. The balance were either what Austin terms "philanthropic" partnerships involving merely arms-length donations or "transactional" partnerships involving broader interactions and some mutual sharing of missions and values but not substantial joint ventures.[11]

A similar conclusion emerges from the interviews and reports drawn on for this report. Most partnerships, as the data above suggested, are largely "philanthropic," involving periodic contributions, usually at a fairly modest level. Thus a study of corporate-nonprofit partnership in Brazil published in 2005 found that "true cross-sectoral partnerships are rare in Brazil."[12] "Generally corporations operate by themselves rather than through civil society," noted another Brazilian insider.[13] Even nonprofits with a considerable track record of success in attracting corporate support complain about the uncertain nature of this support. Un Techo para Chile, for example, a model nonprofit that has attracted more than one hundred corporate sponsors to its mission of mobilizing volunteers to build housing for the poor, still finds the corporate sponsorship "sporadic." Leaders of the organization estimate there are no more than four or five permanent NGO-corporate alliances in Chile. Minuto de Dios, a prominent Catholic charity in Colombia, reported a similar finding. Minuto has built an impressive network of housing, education, and social welfare activities on the base of a variety of alliances. Yet managers of the organization concede that they have to renegotiate private-sector cooperation "project by project."[14] This is consistent with the experience of Pro-Natura, a well-respected nature conservancy organization in Mexico. While the organization benefited early on from the benefaction of two prominent business leaders, it ultimately had to turn to international assistance to survive and can claim only one company that has a "more or less permanent relationship" with it.[15]

Where corporate-nonprofit partnerships develop, moreover, they are often with a narrow band of safe and "respectable" organizations. Research in Argentina, for example, found that corporate donations went mostly to traditional institutions, such as religious institutions, clubs, hospitals, and schools, though nontraditional organizations such as soup kitchens, social-support organizations, and grass-roots organizations have recently come within the corporate purview as well.[16] Many of the stronger partnerships turn out to be with nonprofits created by the businesses. This was the case, for example, with the partnership between

Chile's Banco de Crédito e Inversiones and the nonprofit Corporación de Crédito de Menor, one of the partnerships highlighted in the recent work of the Social Enterprise Knowledge Network. This nonprofit was created by a number of the bank's executives to protect girls at risk; it later evolved into a major nonprofit for at-risk youth.[17] Similarly, the partnership forged by Colombia's Corona Corporation to improve hospital management was with a nonprofit that Corona helped to found—the Centro de Gestión Hospitalaria. When Grupo Corona launched an effort to improve education, it once again did not choose to work through an existing NGO but to create a new structure—a nonprofit organization called Prodencia—to execute education projects. In Brazil, as well, corporations are increasingly establishing their own operating "institutes," bypassing NGOs. This naturally creates a certain tension with the nonprofit organizations operating in these fields.[18]

The Obstacles

How can we explain this relatively limited development of corporate-nonprofit partnerships in Latin America? Clearly a number of factors seem to be at work.

Historic Tension between Business and Civil Society

In the first place, business and civil society have long been at odds in Latin America. As one observer explained, "Chile's Accion RSE historically only worked with businesses and not civil society organizations because of the history of social organizations, which were on the left while business was on the right." "There is very limited experience of cooperation between nonprofit organizations and corporations in Chile," confirms another informed observer. In Colombia, as well, true partnerships between corporations and civil society are limited by what one observer termed "a cultural problem." In particular, "companies have a deep distrust toward NGOs." As one close student of the Latin American philanthropic scene has put it: "Many donors continue to lack a sense of identification or significant involvement with their beneficiaries and do not subscribe to a broader civil society agenda." This reflects a deeper sense of isolation on the part of the Latin business community, a sense that is dissipating but still impedes fully integrated and equal relationships.[19]

These business sentiments are fully reciprocated on the nonprofit side. Nonprofits are deeply suspicious of the motives of corporations in their social responsibility activities, often seeing them as no more than public-relations ploys intended to provide a social face on corporate exploitation or a cover for the negative effects of globalization, but offering little concrete help. This reflects a longstanding suspicion and low esteem for corporations and the entrepreneurial class throughout Latin America. "Corporations in Latin America are much more vulnerable than corporations in the U.S.," explained one prominent Latin business leader. "Public opposition to them is great." "NGOs mistrust enterprises," confirmed one Mexican informant, and a Brazilian expert agreed, noting that civil society organizations (CSOs) in Brazil are "quite ambivalent" about partnerships with corporations. Among the reasons for skepticism cited by Brazilian CSOs were "the incompatibility of the logic and the rhythms of the work, lack of knowledge or sensitivity on the part of the companies, the arrogant and imposing, or the paternalistic and condescending, attitude with which the company relates to the entity, the lack of clarity as to the intentions of the company, and the uncertainty as to the duration of the relationship."[20]

Concerns about Nonprofit Capacity

Complicating the relationship between businesses and civil society further are widespread business doubts not only about the political stance of Latin American nonprofit organizations, but also about their basic efficiency and effectiveness. Notes one corporate official, cooperation is difficult because "civil society is not that impressive. The limitations of civil society are the problem." A survey in Brazil found 25 percent of companies citing lack of trust in CSOs as a reason for reluctance to partner with these organizations. Observers in Mexico similarly report that businesses feel NGOs are inefficient or squander money on administration. While a few companies, such as those supporting the Merced Foundation and its "strength" program in Mexico, have invested in NGO capacity building to overcome this problem, most have not. These programs have therefore had to rely heavily on external support. [21]

The Cult of the Empresa

While doubting the capacity of the nonprofit sector, Latin businesses have developed a heightened sense of their own capacity to produce positive change in their societies, and this has added to their reluctance to throw in their lot with the nonprofit sector. In part this reflects the natural tendency of entrepreneurs to take charge and do things themselves. These sentiments have been exaggerated in the Latin context, however, by frustration with the capacity of both civil society and government to get things done in a context in which perceived dangers to social peace are looming. The result has been the emergence in some quarters of a veritable "cult of the *empresa*," or business firm—a conviction that the region's businesses are the leading agents of social change, indeed, the only agents capable of saving Latin American society from disaster and moving it forward. [22]

This position calls to mind, of course, the "welfare capitalism" movement in early twentieth-century America, during which leaders such as Herbert Hoover anointed "the humane industrialized corporation" as "the chief instrument of social progress" before the Great Depression put such dreams to rest.[23] Whether a similar fate is in store for the modern cult of the *empresa* in the Latin setting is difficult to predict. Clearly, this sentiment has the potential to produce enormous positive consequences, stimulating such groundbreaking business undertakings as Colombia's Empresarios por la Educación or Brazil's Todos pela Educacion. But it also distances the business community from other social actors, reducing these other actors to second-class passengers on the business community's high-speed locomotive. "Corporations believe they have the answers, that they're outsiders to society coming in to offer solutions," notes one corporate foundation leader. "The businesses like to be in control," notes another.[24] The upshot is another barrier to true cross-sector collaboration.

Imperfections in the Collaboration Marketplace

These various tensions complicate what is always one of the greatest challenges in forging partnerships: finding suitable partners. As James Austin has noted, even in the United States "the alliance marketplace . . . is underdeveloped and inefficient."[25] Given the much more severe class divisions in Latin America, these obstacles are multiplied many times. Alliances depend on trust, and trust grows with familiarity. In the context of Latin America, however, the opportunities for interaction between the business community and the nonprofit sector are few and far between. This has created a kind of class system within the nonprofit sector. As one informant put it: "The third sector in Brazil is like Brazilian football—there are different 'leagues'—first, second, third. Only the first league gets media attention and the chance to forge alliances with businesses. The second league plays its games, but largely out of sight and has a hard time breaking through."[26] This may help explain why the organizations that succeed in forming alliances with businesses are so often organizations that the businesses create, that are branches or affiliates of the Catholic Church, or that have some other "angel" who intervenes for them with the business community. In many parts of the region the wives of business leaders perform this "angel" function and thus provide the critical links between civil society and the corporate world. But this still leaves numerous effective nonprofit organizations on the sidelines with little opportunity to tap into the partnership scene.

The Emergence of "Political" Foundations

A final factor complicating the tender relationships between corporations and CSOs in the region has been the emergence of foundations founded by political leaders or, more commonly, the spouses of political leaders. Vamos Mexico, founded by the wife of Vicente Fox in Mexico, and Comunidad Solidaria, founded by the wife of Henrico Cardoza in Brazil, are examples of these. What makes these institutions problematic for the evolving relationships between corporations and CSOs is not that they fail to do good work, but that they tend to siphon off precious resources of time and money that the existing CSOs desperately need. Yet few corporations can resist the wife of a head of state when she comes calling, looking for corporate partnerships with "her" foundation.

Promising Examples

Despite these obstacles, the partnership environment is far from barren in Latin America. To the contrary, there are numerous early flirtations, a number of long-term friendships, and at least a few serious engagements, even if full-scale marriages remain sparse. Among these various relationships are the following:

In Mexico

- Fundación Televisa's cooperation with the UNITEC organization to create a network of media labs to promote reading;
- The partnership, mentioned in the previous chapter, of Fomento Social Banamex, the Instituto para la Planeación del Desarollo (the Institute for Development Planning), and Servicios para el Desarollo (Service for Development) to assist in promoting technology training and broader community development for the citizens surrounding Ixmiquilpan in northern Mexico;
- Danone's partnership with Casa de la Amistad para Niños con Cáncer (Friendship House for Children with Cancer) to ease the plight of child cancer victims; and
- Bimbo bread company's longstanding involvement with Reforestamos Mexico, the NGO it created in 2002 in response to a plea from the government to assist in the reforestation of Mexico City following a devastating forest fire in 1998.

In Brazil

- ABN AMRO Bank's partnership with Friends of the Earth to train the bank's loan officers to assess the environmental risks associated with their loans;
- Phillip Morris Company's arrangement with the Instituto Qualidade no Ensino to manage a package of educational improvements in three Brazilian cities of interest to the company; and

- Fundação Telefônica's partnership with the nonprofit Tenepec to promote Telefônica's Educarede Program aimed at promoting reading by linking students to reading materials via computers.

In Colombia

- Microsoft's cooperation with several nonprofit organizations and with Hewlett-Packard, Compumax, and Argos to create, equip, and operate community technology centers designed to teach disadvantaged people computer skills;
- The cooperation Hocol, ISA (Interconnect Electrica), and other companies have forged with Prodepaz, the CSO that serves as a bridge between companies and communities in conflict zones;
- The Consortium for Community Development formed by a number of Colombian corporate foundations, including Corona, Cartón, Arcor, and Minetti, in the 1990s to foster community-based approaches to development;
- The RedEAmerica network formed by the IAF to foster corporate involvement in community- based development projects; and
- The partnership between Minuto de Dios and Riviende Bank under which the bank offers customers withdrawing money from its Automatic Teller Machines the opportunity to contribute "500 pesos de dios" (about US$0.25 for God).

In Argentina

- The joint venture between *La Nación* newspaper and the nonprofit Red Solidaria outlined in Box 4–1, under which *La Nación* offers a regular feature in its paper through which Red Solidaria can advertise the needs various nonprofits and individuals have for volunteers;
- The support that Fundación Telefonica is providing to Fundación del Viso, a community development organization on the outskirts of Buenos Aires; and
- The cooperation that Gas Ban has forged with Provivenda Social to organize the construction of natural gas lines in a slum area of Buenos Aires.

In Chile

- The substantial support that Banco Santander-Chile provides to the nonprofit Un Teche para Chile (A Roof for Chile) to support this organization's efforts to construct housing for Chile's disadvantaged population.

Conclusion

In short, corporations in Latin America are clearly nibbling at the edges of substantial cross-sectoral partnerships with nonprofit organizations in a wide range of fields. In addition, they are beginning to build quite extraordinary business coalitions to assault some of the region's most intractable long-term problems, such as the basic educational system.

At the same time, an enormous gulf continues to separate the business sector from CSOs in the region, with considerable suspicions on both sides. What is more, few of the collaborations that exist have moved much beyond the "philanthropic" stage. Indeed, there are signs that corporations are increasing their direct activities through special "institutes" and business-only alliances instead of turning more extensively to third-sector partnerships. In fact, many of the more advanced corporate leaders are coming to embrace a virtual cult of the *empresa*, a view of the corporate sector as the ultimate savior of the region.

Nevertheless, there is enough activity in the social partnering space in the region to give at least modest hope that true cross-sector and intra-sectoral partnerships may yet be emerging, however haltingly and unevenly. The emergence of a sizable core of CSR professionals may be facilitating this development by bringing knowledge of the civil-society sector into the corporations and breaking down political and cultural barriers. The emergence of training programs for nonprofit managers may be helping as well, improving the managerial reputation of CSOs. Whether these developments will lead to the blossoming of more extensive and intensive partnerships is anyone's guess. What seems clear, however, is that something like this will be required to gain real traction on the region's serious problems.

Chapter 5

Participation

The one thing no company can outsource is its relationship with the people.
—ROMIRO SANTA, HOCOL CORPORATION

Within two months of its takeover of Hocol S.A., a Colombian oil company, in 1993, Royal Dutch Shell confronted a strike by the community surrounding San Francisco, a small town south of Bogotá where the company had been drilling for a decade. Community residents were fed up and demanded more participation in the affairs of the company. In response, Shell hired a team of consultants to analyze the community's needs and recommend a plan of action. Ultimately, the consultants advised Shell to offer the community a package of educational improvements, a solution that seemed fully consistent with the prevailing "MBA model" of bringing corporate social engagement activities into line with corporate business needs.

When this plan was presented to the community, however, it was rejected out of hand. Instead, community leaders indicated that what they thought the community needed was a cemetery. Perplexed, Hocol's new owner tried a different approach: it reached out to the community and resolved to listen, an unusual posture at the time for Latin American corporations. At a series of meetings, community leaders pointed out that all the careful planning of the consultants was irrelevant to the situation the community was facing, that no amount of educational improvement would be viable until the community achieved a degree of peace, and that this would not be possible until there was a place to bury the numerous bodies that regularly appeared on the community's trails as a consequence of the continued violence raging between local guerrillas and right-wing militias. Without a cemetery the community members had to leave bodies where they fell, lest they be accused by either side of honoring the other side's dead. This made it impossible for children to take the trails to school.[1]

Rise of the Participatory Model

Underlying this story is a crucial issue that has been muted in much of the discourse about CSR, but that the Latin American reality brings vividly into focus. It is the issue of the community role in corporate social engagement.

As we have seen, much of the contemporary mantra of CSR assumes that the task of formulating corporate social engagement strategies belongs chiefly to the corporations, their foundations, and the outside consultants they often hire. It is the job of these worthies to analyze corporate business strategies and formulate corporate social engagement strategies that are most consistent with them. The approach is top down, rather than bottom up, with the corporations in the position of deciding what aspect of their "competitive context" is most in need of improvement, and therefore what it is in their best corporate interest to offer to the communities. The role of communities in this model is to accept what corporations offer and express gratitude for it.

Increasingly, however, an alternative to this "MBA model" of corporate social engagement has surfaced in Latin America. The key feature of this model is the active participation of community residents in the design of corporate social engagement activities.

This "participatory model" grew initially out of the necessities of practice in the all-too-numerous zones of violence in the Colombian interior. Hocol, which "wrote the book" on this approach, discovered that involving residents in decisions affecting their lives was the best protection against the violence that was constantly threatening the firm's operations. It therefore adopted a consciously participatory strategy, encouraging the development of grass-roots leaders and taking advantage of Colombia's innovative 1991 Constitution, which called for the creation of local elected boards, *juntas de accion communal,* in rural areas throughout the country. "Hocol has been teaching the Constitution to the community," noted the leader of Hocol's Transparency and Integrity Team, working with local communities in the areas of its facilities to establish these constitutionally sanctioned local boards and then relying on them to set priorities for the company's social engagement work.[2]

Although Hocol "wrote the book" on this participatory model, it has not been alone in promoting it. Nor is the presence of violence the only rationale for supporting it. Many observers have acknowledged that the poverty and inequality that have characterized Latin American societies are not only economic in character. They are also social and psychological, the product of decades of social dominance that have bequeathed what one observer terms "a climate of submission" that is hardly conducive to robust development, to the formation of a capable work force, or to the kind of self-help needed to overcome poverty and eradicate rampant criminality.[3]

Also pushing in the same direction have been the new strains of development thinking that surfaced in the late 1960s and continued into the 1970s and 1980s as faith in the capacity of state-centered development approaches began to wane. While one outgrowth of this shift in thinking was a dramatic turn to the market and to private direct investment, a second was a stress on engaging poor people in their own development and supporting the grass-roots organizations through which such engagement could be promoted. Indeed, an entire school of development strategy surfaced emphasizing "assisted self-reliance" as the most effective path to poverty alleviation. This approach found support in research findings showing that the development projects with the greatest long-term positive results tended almost universally to involve active beneficiary participation in project design and management, most often through organizations responsive to community control. As one study put it: "Anti-poverty programs that the official political-administrative hierarchy designs and implements in a heavily, almost exclusively top-down fashion tend to be ineffective. Such efforts have a hard time reaching their grassroots clientele through all the intervening bureaucratic layering—and a still harder time engaging local people in the conduct and management of their own poverty alleviation."[4]

This "assisted self-reliance" approach gained special traction in Latin America due to the concerns triggered by the Castro revolution, which underscored the need to reach out more directly to the rural poor. The upshot was a surge of grass-roots organizing spearheaded by a number of unlikely sources, including urban intellectuals frustrated with authoritarian political regimes and disengaged business sectors, U.S. and other international foundations, and a reinvigorated Catholic Church, which sponsored the creation of Christian base communities aimed at promoting local self-development in thousands of rural villages throughout the region.

Left to their own devices, it is unlikely that many corporations would have found their way to participatory development. Indeed, businesses have long been wary of grass-roots empowerment and alienated from the intellectuals promoting it. But fortuitously, Latin American companies were not left wholly to their own devices. A number of diffusion agents surfaced to help lead the way.

One of the most important of these was Hocol itself. Prompted by the severe violence in many of the areas where it was operating, Hocol formulated a program of leadership development, grass-roots organizing, reliance on the local populations for supplies and workers, and close cooperation with the community councils mandated by the Colombian Constitution of 1991. In the process Hocol reconceptualized itself as "A Company that Shares in the Life of Colombia" to emphasize this participatory approach.[5] The payoffs from this approach proved to be substantial; among oil companies, Hocol alone has been able to work in the zones of violence. Over time, other oil companies took notice and began to emulate the practices. In response, Hocol joined with other Colombian oil companies to form the Association of Oil Foundations of Colombia (AFC) and has used this vehicle to help spread the techniques of participatory development.[6] Not surprisingly, companies in other fields began to take notice and to realize that strategies of empowerment might hold the best hope of gaining traction on Latin America's serious problems.

A second important actor helping to diffuse this participatory approach to Latin corporations has been Colombia's Fundación

Social, the institution founded by Jesuit priests in the early 1900s that had evolved by the 1970s into a sprawling complex of social enterprises. Through its Integral Local Development Program, Fundación Sociál moved in the 1980s to formulate a new "developmental" approach to philanthropy designed, as one analysis put it, to "create a model of social intervention that will permit the vulnerable margins of society to become participants in their development."[7] In the process Fundación Sociál sought to bring the business community out of its bunkers, to break down the tendency of businesses to style themselves as outsiders to society bringing in solutions, and to see themselves instead as integral parts of society sharing the problems of the people and working cooperatively to solve them.[8] Hocol's decision to style itself "a company that shares in the life of Colombia" was a direct outgrowth of the missionary work of Fundación Sociál's longtime activist/philosopher Bernardo Toro, who has carried this message to other Colombian corporations as well.

These ideas fell on receptive ears among some of Colombia's more progressive businesses, such as Fundación Corona and Fundación Smurfit Carton. Indeed, these companies had begun their own experimentation with grass-roots approaches to development in the early 1990s and had forged in 1998 their own organization, the Corporación Consorcio para el Desarollo Comunitario, or Consortium for Community Development, to promote the idea.

A third key actor in the spread of the participatory approach to corporate social engagement in Latin America has been the U.S.-based IAF. As noted earlier, the IAF has a long history of support for participatory development and the grass-roots organizations through which it operates in Latin America.[9] As the neo-liberal economic policies gained ascendance in U.S. policy and in the Latin American region in the 1980s and 1990s, turning more of the attention for social problem solving to the corporate sector, however, the IAF conceived the idea of trying to create linkages among the grass-roots organizations with which it had long been working and the emerging corporate philanthropy programs in the region. In a sense, the IAF sought to marry the two competing schools of thought that surfaced in the 1970s and early 1980s out of the collapse of the prevailing top-down, state-centered approaches to development—the dominant one preaching neo-liberal economic policies and greater reliance on business and the market, and the subsidiary one preaching participation of the poor and the need to engage the energies of grass-roots communities in order to make real progress on poverty alleviation. The idea was to entice Latin American businesses to put their talents and resources in the service not only of corporate philanthropy but also of true grass-roots development.

To be sure, the prospects for consummating this marriage and having it yield the offspring it promised were questionable at best. But there were enough embryos already developing to make the effort seem worth trying. The IAF's approach was therefore to work from these existing lives and nurture them with resources and attention. An initial engagement with Venezuela's state-owned oil company, PDVSA, gave credence to the idea. But it was Colombia, perhaps not surprisingly, that offered especially attractive opportunities through which to advance the experiment. Thus, in 1995 the IAF sponsored the Cartagena Conference and made a matching grant to Colombia's Fundación Corona to establish a fund, the Development Assistance Fund, to finance income-generation projects carried out by grass-roots development organizations in poor areas of Bogotá. In 1996 it awarded $81,000 to Fundación Amanecer, created by a consortium of oil companies, including Hocol, committed to promoting local, self-help development in the eastern part of the country. In 1997 it granted $489,000 to the Asociación Colombiana del Petróleo (ACP) as a match for $990,000 in oil industry funds to help Hocol work with other oil companies to create the Colombian Alliance of Oil Industry Foundations and establish a Small Projects Fund to finance grass-roots development projects carried out by local communities.[10]

Nor was Colombia the only site where this strategy was unfurled. In 1996 the IAF joined forces with the foundation created by Arcor, Argentina's multinational candy producer, to create FEPIC (the Fund for Training, Education, Prevention, and Community Integration) designed to strengthen the capabilities of community-based NGOs in five Argentine provinces. This partnership represented ARCOR's first exposure to grass-roots development, and it ended up fundamentally altering Fundación ARCOR's operation, moving it from an ad hoc, scattered philanthropic approach to a more focused, community-development-oriented investment approach. A similar grant to Fundación Minetti, formed by Grupo Minetti, a major Argentine cement manufacturer, led to the creation of the Building Bridges Fund, which financed grass-roots development organizations in Córdoba.[11]

Building on these and other experiences, the IAF moved in 2002 to forge a more active network of corporate foundations committed to the participatory model of business social engagement and to enlarge the pool of corporations involved. The resulting RedEAmérica network, which now numbers sixty members in twelve countries, has become a dynamic center of support for the participatory approach in the region. Through this network the IAF has disseminated its "Grassroots Development Framework" for measuring project results and has underwritten two additional initiatives, a training effort housed in Colombia's Fundación Corona and a learning network housed in Argentina's Fundación Minetti. As just one indication of the influence this work is having, one RedEAmérica initiative recently secured $9 million from the IDB to promote productive projects engaging local communities.[12]

Finally, the participatory approach to corporate social engagement in Latin America has also benefited from the involvement of a number of important nonprofit intermediary organizations. For example, one of these, Colombia's Prodepaz (Peace and Development Network), serves as a kind of broker between local communities of excluded groups and the powerful forces in business and government that are shaping their future, with the objective of creating a shared vision of the future and a set of concrete initiatives through which to get there. Prodepaz essentially does this by creating "public spaces," occasions for structured conversations between communities and corporations. Its work has attracted a number of key business leaders, especially those in industries that are susceptible to the country's surging violence, such as electricity transmission companies, extractive industries, and firms that need access to the country's natural resources over an extended period, such as the palm-oil industry.[13]

Another nonprofit that has played a significant role in promoting a more participatory style of corporate social engagement is Brazil's Instituto para o Desenvolvimento do Investimento Social (Institute for the Development of Social Investment—IDIS), headed by former Kellogg Foundation regional coordinator

Marcos Kisil. IDIS functions as a technical-assistance adviser to corporate philanthropy programs, promoting participatory approaches and working with companies at the local level to implement them.

The Participatory Model in Practice

Four examples illustrate how this participatory model operates and how it differs from other forms of corporate social engagement.

Klabin[14]

Klabin is Brazil's largest producer and exporter of paper products, including packaging paper, corrugated boxes, and industrial sacks. Because paper production is an industry with a typically heavy environmental and social footprint, one might expect Klabin to have been caught up in the winds of environmental and social concern sweeping through Brazil in the 1990s. But well into the new century Klabin remained a corporate backwater, a traditional family-owned company operating in fifteen isolated communities with a highly dependent population and work force that appeared satisfied with the company's ad hoc social-assistance mode, or at least had little opportunity to change it.

But early in the new century the company encountered serious economic problems and had to sell off a number of its assets. New leadership on the board recognized that the company's international image as an exploiter of forests needed to change. It therefore made a bold leap and reached outside its existing personnel to recruit Wilberto Luiz Lima, Jr.,—a corporate communications director from another company who had earned a reputation as an innovator of social programs—to become Klabin's first director of communications and social responsibility and a member of the corporation's management committee. It is very likely that the board did not know what it was in for.

In quick succession Lima proposed two major innovations: first, that Klabin transform itself from an environmental deadbeat into an environmental leader; and second, that the company give a more coherent structure to its ad hoc and unfocused philanthropic efforts.

To make headway on the first of these innovations, Lima convinced the Klabin board to bring the company into compliance with a new set of forestry preservation standards developed by the Forest Stewardship Council (FSC), an independent certifying organization that monitors planting and preservation of forests throughout the world. As a result, Klabin was the first company in the world to obtain FSC certification for three of its paper and packaging products, and, by the beginning of 2007, certification was achieved for all of Klabin's paper products.

To make headway on the second objective, Lima took an even more unorthodox approach. He retained Brazil's IDIS to help the company decide how to spend an $11 million fund that Brazil's National Bank of Social and Economic Development required Klabin to invest in community improvements as part of a loan that the bank extended to the company to finance a major expansion project at its plant in Telêmaco Borba. Rather than conduct the typical top-down needs assessment, IDIS urged Lima to adopt an unconventional participatory approach and throw the decisions into the hands of local residents. The Klabin board initially

---

Box 5–1. Klabin Telêmaco Borba Initiative

Ronaldo woke up every day except Sunday at 5 a.m. His father had typically already showered and had breakfast. But Ronaldo was dog tired this particular morning. The previous night he had sat together with his new community work group until 1 a.m. They had intensively discussed proposals for the best way to invest the money that would come to the community as a result of the expansion of Klabin's plant in Telêmaco Borba. Klabin had secured a credit worth US$1 billion from the Brazilian National Bank of Social and Economic Development, and a condition of the loan was that 1 percent of this money had to be reinvested in the community. Last week twenty-two people met to discuss this issue. As a result of that meeting they had founded working groups. Ronaldo was in the infrastructure group. The members did not know the budget, but there were several things to do. Ronaldo was proud to be a member, and his father was proud, too. He was the third generation of his family to work for Klabin. The family members were real *Klabineros*, and thanks to this investment, his son would also have a future in Telêmaco Borba.

resisted this idea, but Lima was ultimately able to persuade it. The upshot was a two-year process of discovery and community organizing involving community surveys; in-depth consultations with local residents; the formation of a community-based steering committee involving Klabin employees, local municipal leaders, and civil society representatives that formulated a set of strategies; and the creation by this group of six working groups to formulate concrete projects in such areas as water and environment; entrepreneurship; and culture, sports, and leisure.

The whole process seems to have generated a burst of enthusiasm among longtime residents. "I came very much in touch with my neighbors," noted one participant. "I feel integrated, and I'm more active than I was before." (See Box 5–1.)

Hocol[15]

If Klabin provides an example of a newcomer to participatory corporate social engagement, Hocol, as already indicated, offers an example with a more fully developed history. A relatively small producer by world standards, Hocol is a Colombian corporation that has passed through a succession of foreign owners. Operating as it does in some of the most troubled regions in the country, Hocol evolved a business strategy in the mid 1990s that put a premium on establishing solid working relationships with the communities in which its facilities are located. Indeed, the company underwent an internal "reflection process" that led to the articulation of an integrated concept of its relationship to these communities. "We are a citizen enterprise," reads the document that resulted from this process, "and therefore, we accept the rights and constitutional duties as citizens of this country. . . . Our purpose is to be part of the country, to stay and to share a long-term business, generating wealth and opportunities for all, within the framework of the political Constitution, and honouring human rights and a dignified living as our north [star]."[16]

Consistent with this extraordinary political testament, Hocol has renounced the use of arms in its dealings with local violence; it tries to hire all its workers and most of its contractors in the areas in which it operates, and it steers away from social programs that might be considered paternalistic or simply philanthropic. Most important for our purposes here, Hocol, as noted above, makes vigorous efforts to foster community participation, making active use of the *juntas de acción communal* called for in the 1991 Colombian Constitution and committing itself to communicating its own plans and programs to community residents.

Hocol had an unusual opportunity to demonstrate its adherence to these principles when it began oil explorations in 2001–2 near the small town of Tesalia in the Huila department of Colombia, where the company has most of its operations. Aware that a discovery of oil in the area would alter the region considerably, Hocol launched a process of community dialogues to seek input from the local community about how it wished to invest whatever wealth might be generated as a result. Structured meetings were held with various segments of the population—coffee growers, cattle raisers, senior citizens, women, religious groups, and local political officials. The company educated the citizenry about oil royalties and fostered a dialogue about investment priorities. Out of this process emerged a plan of action calling for mechanisms of citizen participation, control of public expenditure, improvements in the water and sewage system, a scholarship program for local young people, and other priorities. Perhaps most important, the process demonstrated the ability of a population with limited formal education and almost no prior experience with participation to take an active role in its future. It was thus profoundly empowering for the community, while helping to ensure the company a stable place in which to operate for years to come.

Holcim Ortópolis Program[17]

Holcim Brazil, a subsidiary of a huge international cement and concrete manufacturer based in Switzerland, followed a similar route to its commitment to a participatory approach to corporate social engagement. In 1996, as part of its Plano Brazil, Holcim bought Grupo Cimento Paraiso, a Brazilian family firm with cement plants in four communities, including the town of Barroso. The Barroso plant had already shrunk from 1,210 employees in the 1980s to 650 when Holcim bought it, and Holcim then introduced an automation process that reduced that number to 150 in only half a year. Since the former owners had lived in the town and were paternalistic philanthropists, sponsoring festivities and family gatherings, the contrast with the big, bad, uncaring multinational firm was stark, causing Holcim's standing in the community to plummet.

Rather than turning its back on this situation or responding defensively, Holcim, inspired by the IAF RedEAmérica consortium, which it joined, launched the Ortópolis or Sustainable City program, a participatory development process aimed at establishing a consensus model of Barrosa's future as a sustainable city. With the aid of Edgar von Buettner, an outside consultant, Holcim convened a community-planning group, which quickly established nine working groups to identify action priorities for the community. These groups focused on topics such as the establishment of a micro-credit program for small entrepreneurs, agricultural development efforts, and ecological projects (see Box 5–2).

With partial support from IAF, Holcim was then able to establish a development fund to help underwrite some of these

---

Box 5–2. The Holcim Ortópolis Project

When Luisa heard of Holcim's call for participants to discuss ideas for a sustainable future for her town of Barroso, she was not willing to believe that this could change anything. She did not trust Holcim, the multinational company that had taken over the cement factory—the town's biggest employer—in 1996. its first action had been to dismiss five hundred people. Why should it suddenly worry about the community's development? But Luisa was also president of the local NGO Futuro para nossos miúdos (Future for Our Children), and she felt a responsibility at least to investigate the consequences of Holcim's decisions in Barroso. The meeting took place in September 2003 and was scheduled for a whole day. Luisa went with reluctance—and was totally surprised. Invited were not only the opinion leaders in Barroso; the group comprised forty people, from ordinary people from the street to the mayor. The group intensively brainstormed about community issues. It developed nine action groups and elected a coordinator for each. Luisa went to the entrepreneur group that aimed to develop the local community with micro-credits for small family enterprises. Now, nearly four years later, the program has helped eleven families to start up businesses such as a pottery or a kindergarten for working mothers. The group still meets monthly and, despite the fact that some people have left and others have joined, all of its members are united in the will to change something and the experience of doing so.

activities. Thus, a micro-credit fund was established that stimulated eleven family businesses in its first four years. To make the process permanent, moreover, an ongoing planning structure was put in place in the form of a new community organization, the Associação Ortópolis Barroso.

Banamex Marginal Communities Initiative[18]

While the previous examples of corporate support for grassroots development all featured essentially extractive industries with a need to make peace with communities in the vicinity of their operations, a quite different example is presented by the experience of the Mexican bank Banamex in its work in the mountainous region around Ixmiquilpan north of Mexico City. The business tie between this remote area and Banamex is indirect at best. It seems doubtful, therefore, that the MBA model of corporate social engagement would have led to a meaningful commitment of Banamex time and talents to this area. Indeed, Banamex's new owner, Citigroup, may already be questioning the venture.

Three factors motivated Banamex to get involved in a grassroots development project in faraway Aquas Blancas and more than thirty similar forgotten "marginal" areas. First, then Mexican president Vicente Fox launched a major initiative to promote development in over 250 of Mexico's poorest communities, and he invited Banamex, along with other major corporations, to join forces with the government in the initiative. This illustrates the critical catalytic role that government can play as a stimulus to corporate social involvement in Latin America, particularly in Mexico, where deference to the state remains strong. Second, Fernando Peón Escalante, executive director of the Fomento Sociál Banamex, had a long history of involvement with issues of poverty in Mexico through his former role as a civil servant in the Mexican government; he consequently was inclined to respond positively to this invitation. Escalante is an unusual corporate social engagement official, more social worker than MBA graduate in his outlook. Finally, and critically, the project had the personal support of Banamex's CEO, Alfredo Harp. Indeed, the financial support for the effort is being provided by Harp personally rather than the bank institutionally. It turns out that Harp had been a victim of Mexico's urban violence ten years earlier, having been kidnapped and ultimately ransomed and released. The experience changed his life and gave him a special appreciation of the need for corporate social engagement to change the long-term prospects for Mexico's poor.

Once it decided to accept the invitation to participate in Vicente Fox's Marginal Communities Initiative, Banamex approached the task with considerable ingenuity. The heart of the government's program was an effort to introduce training in computer literacy for youth in these marginal communities. The government thus forged an alliance with the Latin American Institute for Educational Communication (ILSE) under which ILSE would deliver six thousand computers to the 277 communities involved in the effort and install related equipment to connect the computers to the Internet. The Department of Education, in turn, would provide educational programs to instruct community residents in the use of the computers. The communities were asked to supply a physical structure to house the equipment and provide space for training community residents. The corporations were asked to help finance these facilities and cover the costs of their personnel.

Banamex went well beyond what the government requested, however, supplementing the technology provided by ILSE with additional equipment secured from Hewlett-Packard and integrating the program into a broader strategy of community empowerment. To achieve this, Banamex wisely reached out to professionals in the community development field. First, it retained the Instituto para la Planeación del Desarrollo (Institute for Development Planning—IPD), an NGO with twenty-five years of experience doing technical assistance and planning work in marginal communities in the country, historically in cooperation with the Mexican Ministry of Social Development. IPD was assigned the task of formulating a strategy for Banaméx's involvement with the Marginal Communities Initiative. IPD, in turn, reached out to the network of grass-roots NGOs with which it regularly works in Mexico's marginal regions. In the vicinity of Aguas Blancas, one of the communities in which Banaméx agreed to work, for example, IPD had a working relationship with Servicio para el Desarrollo, A.C. (Service for Development—SEDAC), a twenty-five-year-old grass-roots development organization created and still operated by a former priest, Salvador

Garcia, and his wife, a former nun, and supported in its early days, interestingly enough, by the IAF.

With the support of IPD and Banaméx, and the impetus and facility provided by the government-sponsored computer-training program, SEDAC has set about building a viable community organization embracing five communities in the hills surrounding the town of Ixmiquilpan. The focal point of this effort is the training center financed by the joint Banaméx-government program to promote computer literacy in this remote region. In addition to the training director, this facility has a full-time community planner and houses a new revolving-loan fund managed by a committee of community residents (most of them women, because the men in the area have had to migrate to the United States or Mexico City to find work). This fund has given critical management training to local residents, boosting their self-confidence and introducing them to basic business principles. In the process it has helped infuse some needed funds into local small businesses—for example, underwriting the cost of a refrigerator for a small store, of livestock for a farmer, of a grinder for a corn restaurant, and of an oven for a bakery. As one member of the revolving loan fund committee explained: "The banks won't make loans to us in this area. They charge interest and have a lot of requirements. The revolving loan approach is better for us. People pay back these loans without prompting." Another noted: "We've learned a lot through this project. I've even learned how to do public speaking."

Conclusion

In short, a corporate social engagement model that goes well beyond the standard "MBA paradigm" has surfaced in Latin America. This community-based or participatory model is more long-term and problem focused in its orientation and places the corporation in a different posture toward the community—not as an outsider projecting answers or offering assistance, but as an insider sharing the hard work of searching for solutions. Instead of beginning from the corporation and what it needs from its "competitive context," this approach begins from the community and what it needs to thrive in cooperation with the company. Finally, the approach involves a significant empowerment dimension, providing not simply resources and/or services but also skills, self-confidence, and institutional structures that can alter both the social and economic dimensions of disadvantage over the long run.

How widespread this model has become in the region is difficult to determine. Certainly there are more examples than have been detailed here. Many companies, such as Telefônica de Argentina, Aguas Argentinas before the recent take-over of its French parent company by the government, and Natural Gas Ban, have begun giving local communities a larger voice in projects that affect them. Yet the range of companies that have so far embraced this approach remains small, and the classic MBA approach remains more widespread. The participatory model appeals most to companies operating in isolated settings where community support is critical to company operations. Hence, extractive industries or companies dependent on a particular raw material are the most active adherents. In addition to a lack of incentive, most companies also lack the technical capacity to relate to communities in an effective way. Although they could seek help from community-based NGOs, as Banamex has done, the perception of business among the community-based NGOs has been skeptical at best, as we will see more fully below. As a consequence, the top-down approach remains far more prevalent, leaving most companies "living in a forest," as one observer put it. Whether the RedEAmérica network and other similar efforts to spread the participatory model can reverse this situation remains to be seen. From the evidence at hand, however, there seems at least some basis for hope.

Chapter 6

Penetration

The key is when corporations take corporate social respon-
sibility seriously in the operation of their businesses.
—Sergio Haddad, ABONG, Brazil

We do the business differently.
—Maria Emilia Correa, Masisa, Chile

Ronaldinho Chervere has operated his small farm since 1992, mainly planting corn. He founded it with his wife and has culti-vated it with their four children. Their business did not make them rich. It was enough to live on, and nothing more. They had un-used acres, but there was no way to use the fallow land. They did not have the money to buy equipment, and the banks would not give them credit. They had no security, and the farming business was very unreliable. The previous year a worm had destroyed 50 percent of their harvest. This was not necessary because there were seeds on the market that were resistant. But they were far more expensive. Another problem was the humidity where they stored the corn. It made Chervere feel sick when he thought about how much of their hard work was wasted every year.

When the huge American supermarket chain Wal-Mart came into town, Chervere did not feel relieved. Wal-Mart would buy its products from wholesalers, so there would be no connection to his meager business. But to his surprise, one day a salesman from this big chain came to his farm for a chat. The salesman asked sev-eral questions about his production, and he told Ronaldinho that Wal-Mart was following a regional approach. It would attempt to

87

include local farmers and businesses among its suppliers, but it would need reliable partners. Ronaldinho knew what this meant, and he doubted that his small business would be able to comply. But the man told him that Wal-Mart had a Producers' Club. He would get the chance to improve his farming practice through credits and a knowledge network. Ronaldinho decided to join the club, and he has never regretted it. With Wal-Mart as a client, he obtained the needed credits. Through the network he learned new practices to deal with the tropical humidity that was ruining his crop. Last year he won a prize for the best performing farm in the northeast of Brazil, and it gave him great pride.

Ronaldinho's story is the newest face of corporate social engagement in Latin America. This new face goes well beyond all three forms of corporate philanthropy recently identified by Michael Porter and Mark Kramer in the pages of the *Harvard Business Review*—"communal obligation" (support of civic or welfare organizations out of a desire to be a good citizen); "good will building" (contributions designed to improve a company's relationships); and even "strategic giving" (contributions focused on enhancing a firm's competitive context). All three of these essentially involve "giving money to other organizations that actually deliver the social benefits."[1] The new face of corporate social engagement differs sharply from this. Instead of making social engagement something *external* to the firm, it involves the *penetration* of social engagement into the *internal* operations of the firm, into its business functions and its product lines. "Masisa does not have a single [social engagement] project," explains one strong exponent of this approach. "The whole business strategy is the project."[2]

The new term increasingly gaining acceptance to depict this internalized concept of corporate social engagement is *corporate sustainability*. This term has been advanced by the World Business Council for Sustainable Development (WBCSD) to promote business attention to the social and environmental impact of its business actions, and the theme has been taken up by prominent Latin American corporate leaders such as GrupoNueva's Stephan Schmidheiny and Julio Moura. As articulated recently by Moura, who serves as vice president of the WBCSD, this strategy goes well beyond not only corporate philanthropy but also corporate social responsibility. It encourages businesses not only to address the challenges of the twenty-first century through their charitable

firms in Latin America to seek compliance with ISO standards in the quality control and environmental areas as well.[7]

Also influential is the Global Reporting Initiative (GRI), a set of sustainability reporting guidelines formulated through a broad consensus process and widely utilized by corporations to communicate their economic, environmental, and social performance. Many of the corporations in Latin America that are producing social reports have turned to the GRI standards because of their status as a recognizable stamp of approval at the international level.

What gives these standards force, of course, are the competitive pressures they create for corporations to adhere to them. As Mexican businessman Manuel Arango observed, "Setting standards is important because then the corporations compete to meet them."[8] For this to occur, however, there must be avant-garde business leaders willing to take the first step and thus create the competitive pressures on others to comply.

Fortunately, Latin America has found such leaders. One of the earliest was Fabio Barbosa of ABN AMRO Real Bank in Brazil. ABN AMRO Real Bank was formed in 1998 out of the merger of ABN AMRO Bank, a branch of the Dutch financial giant, and Brazil's Banco Real. As noted earlier, to forge the two entities into a single unit, Barbosa, the CEO of the newly merged firm, determined to foster a new corporate culture around the theme of "a new bank for a new society." Central to this theme was the idea of a bank that created value for its community and thus internalized in its business operations the value-creating impulses embodied in its social engagement activities, including concern for the environment and for the poor. In short, Barbosa determined to make the thoroughgoing penetration of social objectives into the business functions of the firm the defining feature of the new company. This essentially turns the MBA model on its head; instead of having business needs define social objectives, social objectives define business behavior.[9]

Initially, bank managers were stumped about how a bank could manifest its social and environmental commitments in its business activities due to the fact that banks have a relatively limited environmental footprint. But then they had an epiphany. While the bank itself might not have a sizable social or environmental impact, the projects it finances certainly do. If environmental impacts could be incorporated into the bank's loan risk criteria, then the impact could be substantial, especially if other banks followed suit. What is more, the bank could do the same with other types of risk criteria, for example, those relating to social impacts, hiring practices, and training for the disadvantaged.

Armed with this insight, bank officials approached the non-profit Friends of the Earth, which had expertise in assessing environmental risks, to assist it in developing a set of environmental risk criteria and to train bank loan officers in the application of these criteria. The bank also developed similar risk criteria for social impacts, such as sensitivity to workplace safety and business hiring practices. ABN AMRO Real was thus soon able to advertise itself as a new kind of bank, sensitive to the environmental and the social impacts of its lending, and unwilling to do business with polluters or exploiters.

A similar telling example was provided by GrupoNueva, the firm founded by Swiss millionaire Stephan Schmidheiny. In the 1990s uncontrolled clear-cutting of forests and lack of meaningful regulation led to the creation by a coalition of environmentalists and industrialists of the Forest Stewardship Council, which developed a set of standards for sustainable lumber operations. These standards were ultimately widely adopted for forestry operations in the industrialized world, but their adoption in emerging markets largely failed. Schmidheiny determined to turn this around by demonstrating that a sustainable—that is, socially and environmentally responsible—forest products company could operate successfully in an emerging market like Latin America, and that local consumers would respond positively to the idea.[10]

Accordingly, in 2004 GrupoNueva acquired Masisa, a Chilean-based Latin American furniture company, and quickly began to alter its modus operandi. For one thing, it opened a dialogue with the native Indians residing in the areas of Masisa's logging operations, bringing to its dealings with the indigenous population the kind of participatory approach that Hocol had pioneered in Colombia (as described in the previous chapter). Working with the Chilean NGO Casa de la paz (House of Peace), Masisa's new owners undertook intensive stakeholder inquiries to determine the needs of the local population and to devise a strategy of social improvement. As part of this, it redesigned Masisa's logging operations to minimize damage to the local terrain and to comply with the Forest Stewardship Council's standards for replanting and forest management. GrupoNueva also instituted new procedures for handling the carcinogenic formaldehyde that is used in the production of furniture, becoming the only Latin American producer to comply with the European Union standards on this chemical.

To make sure these concepts truly penetrated its business operations, Masisa also established the position of general manager of social and environmental sustainability and gave the official occupying this position a direct reporting line to the CEO. Each plant, in turn, has a person responsible for social and ecological issues who reports to this official. A "sustainability score card" system has also been put in place to assess the social and environmental performance of managers. The result is a thoroughgoing integration of social and environmental concerns into the core operations of the business. As Masisa's sustainability manager puts it: "Companies should not try to use corporate foundations to cover for the things they have not done, like not polluting, or establishing serious respectful relations with stakeholders. You must ask yourself, how do you make money and then build your social engagement into that. . . . This is not a project. We do the business differently."[11]

Masisa and ABN AMRO Real are not the only companies to begin operating in a sustainable manner, however. Other companies have moved in this direction as well. Thus, as noted earlier, when Brazilian-based Klabin Corporation, South America's largest paper recycler, hired its first communications and corporate social responsibility officer in 2002, one of this official's first actions was to push the company to adopt the new Forest Stewardship Council standards. Mexico's Grupo Modelo, a major producer of beer, has also taken pains to integrate environmental concerns into its production processes, putting systems in place in its plants to transform the byproducts of its production into biodegradable materials in compliance with ISO environmental standards. Similarly, Banco Galicia has followed a similar course to ABN AMRO Real in adopting socially and environmentally conscious risk criteria for its lending.[12]

More generally, social reporting has become increasingly widespread, at least among major companies. As noted earlier, over six hundred Brazilian companies regularly report to Instituto Ethos on a broad range of CSR practices, including many related to their basic production processes. Research in Argentina in late

2003 found 44 percent of leading companies working on "social reports." Over 250 Argentine companies have joined the Global Compact, which commits them to work toward achievement of the UN Millennium Development Goals and to prepare annual communiques of progress.[13]

To be sure, many of the companies preparing such reports are doing so as a public-relations operation. What is more, most of those involved are large multinationals with substantial stakes in being able to report to consumers in developed economies that they are operating responsibly in emerging markets, and to have this certified by some respected external body. The real challenge will be to extend the process to small- and medium-sized enterprises. Nevertheless, the integration of social and environmental objectives into business production processes, though slow, is quite real.

Supply-Chain Management

A second major vehicle for the penetration of corporate social engagement objectives into core business practices is through supply-chain management. Supply-chain management is the conscious use of a firm's supply network and subcontracting arrangements to advance corporate social engagement goals. This can take two different forms. The first is the affirmative use of supply-chain decisions to open opportunities to disadvantaged individuals and communities. The second is the regulatory use of supply-chain decisions to penalize suppliers that fail to comply with environmental or social objectives, thus ensuring that a company's suppliers adhere to social norms that the company is attempting to apply in its own business practices and social engagement work.

One of the most vivid examples of this penetration of social concerns into business operations through supply-chain management in the Latin American context is provided, unexpectedly enough, by Wal-Mart, a firm that has not generally been renowned for its social consciousness around the world. However, in its Brazilian operation, Wal-Mart has developed a sophisticated supply-chain management operation that incorporates a variety of advanced precepts of corporate social responsibility.[14]

Like so much of corporate social engagement, the motivations for Wal-Mart Brazil's supply-chain strategy are both moral and material. On the one hand, the corporation has a global mission to "give back to communities." On the other hand, the social and economic conditions that the company faced in its Brazil operations made concerted attention to its supply chain virtually mandatory.

Wal-Mart entered the Brazil market with four stores in 1995 and added another thirty locations over the ensuing nine years. It then went through a major expansion in 2004 and 2005 with the acquisition of another 258 stores from competing chains. Wal-Mart quickly encountered a challenge, however, because Brazil did not offer the conditions that Wal-Mart's U.S.-based business model depended on, namely, its ability to buy huge amounts of quality products and transport them over reliable and low-cost transportation systems for sale in large, accessible retail and wholesale outlets to a broad-based consumer market. Wal-Mart's strategy is successful only in a democratic country with a broad consumer market. Neither of these conditions was fully present in Brazil.

Wal-Mart Brazil therefore set out to alter the situation. One facet of its approach was to launch a corporate foundation, Instituto Wal-Mart, to work on overcoming the social exclusion and widespread impoverishment limiting the size of the consumer market in Brazil, largely through investments in income-generating projects. But far more important for our purposes here was a second strategy managed by the firm's sustainability department. This strategy focused on what is perhaps Wal-Mart's greatest potential source of impact: its influence over the supply chain that is the heart of its whole operation. In particular, as highlighted in the vignette that opened this chapter, the company adopted a regionalization strategy to develop local suppliers in each of the regions in which it has stores. Accordingly, Wal-Mart formed Producers' Clubs in each region to locate, recruit, train, and help equip indigenous suppliers for the full range of the chain's products and to work with these suppliers to improve their quality and reliability. At the same time, the firm combined these positive incentives with restrictions intended to enforce social and environmental standards on its suppliers. Thus, it committed itself to purchase only fair-trade products, that is, products produced with adequate pay, adult labor, and good safety practices, and it developed procedures to verify this. In addition, it formulated standards of environmental performance to ensure that suppliers minimize waste and utilize environmentally friendly processes. To reinforce these practices, moreover, the firm established sustainability objectives for each of its departments, required each department to identify sustainability goals for each product, and made efforts to sensitize its managers and employees both to the sustainability objectives and to the indigenous supply-chain management and regionalization strategy through regular training focused squarely on this topic. Finally, to buttress this effort further, Wal-Mart created a special office to promote the export of products produced by its indigenous Brazilian suppliers to Wal-Mart stores elsewhere in the world in order to promote even broader economic development in Brazil.

While still in its early stages, this strategy is already reaping results. By mid 2007 the Producers' Clubs had fostered 324 small companies providing goods to Wal-Mart regional outlets. In several areas Wal-Mart has teamed up with local nonprofits to help in its dealings with local suppliers. One of these, for example, is Artesanato Solidário (Artesol), which is working with Wal-Mart to supply fair-trade Brazilian arts and crafts, which Wal-Mart Brazil is selling through its Brazilian outlets and introducing in other Wal-Mart locations. Artesol features this partnership on its website, noting, "We would like to have more retailers knocking on our door like this."[15]

Other Latin American firms have also taken affirmative steps to utilize their supply-chain management to promote indigenous economic development. At times, this is deliberate and carefully planned out, as is the case with the elaborate efforts made by Alpina, a Colombian milk-products company, to assist the 450 farms that supply it with milk to operate effectively and environmentally. At other times, it can be serendipitous, as was the case with the Brazilian cosmetics firm O Boticário, which discovered that the natural woven baskets it had decided to purchase from a Thailand supplier for use by shoppers in its hundreds of retail outlets throughout the world could be produced by an artisan cooperative that the firm's foundation had helped to create in the Brazilian rain forest. The company's board quickly agreed to use the indigenous supplier, even though the cost was substantially

higher. The success of this venture subsequently inspired O Boticário to create an Eco-Development Fund in cooperation with the IAF to provide small grants for projects that advance community economic development in environmentally sensitive ways.[16]

The decision by ABN AMRO Real Bank (discussed earlier) to impose social and environmental performance requirements on its 150 suppliers also falls into this category, as does the similar effort by Banco Galicia in Argentina to formulate a Code of Ethics for its two thousand suppliers and require the suppliers to sign a statement of compliance with the code. The Argentine-based candy company Arcor has taken similar steps, incorporating an ethical code into its standard contract with suppliers and initiating a process to interview suppliers on a range of business practices from child-labor through environmental impact.[17] In each of these cases the firm is actively using its influence over its suppliers to promote its social engagement goals, thus using its core business operations to promote its social engagement objectives.

Social Product Development

In addition to changes in production processes and active supply-chain management, a third notable mechanism through which social engagement principles are penetrating Latin American business operations is what might be termed social product development, that is, the development and marketing of products that are specially designed for disadvantaged populations or that promote a social or environmental objective. This form of penetration of social objectives into business operations takes its inspiration from the work of C. K. Pralahad, who has called attention to the enormous economic market represented by the "bottom of the pyramid" and urged companies to target this market with products that will lower costs to purchasers while still earning profits for the companies.[18]

This form of merger of business and social objectives has a history in Latin America, perhaps reflecting the influence of Catholic social doctrines emphasizing solidarity. Whatever the origins, the region has long exhibited a variety of mixed forms of enterprise.

These have been especially evident in Colombia, which pioneered the concept of the *fundación propieteria* (proprietary foundation)—a foundation that owns and operates commercial

businesses, the profits from which are devoted to social purposes. The earliest of these was Fundación Sociál, the social foundation (mentioned in Chapter 1) that was created by a Jesuit priest early in the twentieth century to provide educational opportunities for children. Though supported in part by charitable gifts, Fundación Sociál developed an extensive array of business ventures in construction, banking, insurance, leasing, and communications—many of them operated on cooperative principles, and all of them devoting a significant share of their profits to support the foundation's social mission. In the process Fundación Sociál helped to establish a compelling precedent for socially responsible business in the country. By the 1990s the foundation's network of enterprises included nineteen companies employing ten thousand people and controlling US$3.5 billion in assets.[19]

Fundación FES, created by a group of university professors in Cali, Colombia, to manage a sizable grant from the Ford Foundation in the mid 1960s, followed in Fundación Sociál's footsteps, evolving by the 1990s into a sizable financial institution that utilized its profits to finance a variety of social programs. Fundación FES essentially served as the banker to Colombia's emerging civil society sector, holding grants provided by Northern donors in dollars and then paying them out in depreciated Colombian pesos and collecting fees for its efforts. In the process it captured revenue for Colombian social programs that would otherwise have ended up in the vaults of commercial banks.

Yet another example of Colombia's creative blending of social action and business enterprise is offered by the *caja de compensación* (compensation funds). Initiated in the 1950s by members of the Colombian chamber of industries as an alternative to a government-run and tax-financed social security system, the compensation funds have evolved into enormous social enterprises operating hundreds of social ventures and supplying cash payments for needy families and pensions for elderly workers. For example, Colsubsidio, the largest of what are now fifty-one such compensation funds, operates thirty supermarkets and one hundred drug stores in and around Bogotá in addition to micro-credit facilities, health clinics, and educational institutions. The initial voluntary corporate contributions to these funds were made mandatory in 1957, but today they account for only 30 percent of

Colsubsidio's revenues. The rest comes from the businesses the organization operates.[20]

Closer to the contemporary "bottom of the pyramid" concept is the work of another Colombian institution, the Carvajal Foundation of Cali. This foundation is one of the oldest in Colombia, having been created in 1961 through the donation by the Carvajal family of a 35.5 percent stake in the family's businesses. With these resources the Carvajal Foundation has launched an innovative series of social development programs in the poorest region of Cali. One of the most imaginative of these has been a housing program that featured the construction of a warehouse in the middle of a squatter area to provide space for manufacturers to sell construction materials directly to residents at wholesale prices. In addition, this program developed a modular-housing product that allowed residents to build dwellings room by room as resources allowed. By convincing the city administration to set up an office in the warehouse, where residents could quickly obtain building permits, and enticing the government-owned Central Mortgage Bank to open an office in this same facility, the foundation was able to stimulate a robust "bottom of the pyramid" business venture that produced enormous social benefits for homeless slum dwellers.[21]

These early Latin American examples of adapting business activities to social purposes have now been joined by a variety of contemporary examples. One of the most vivid is the Ekos product line developed by the Brazilian cosmetics firm Natura beginning in 2000. Natura found a way to convert the natural substances used by traditional indigenous communities in the Brazilian hinterlands into a marketable product line that at one and the same time advances the cause of Brazilian bio-diversity (by using substances drawn from the region's natural flora) and generates social and economic wealth for the indigenous communities (by employing local artisans to harvest the raw material and assist in making the finished products). The success of this product line has given jobs to hundreds of people while encouraging the protection of the natural wetlands.[22]

A somewhat different example is offered by the experience of Gas Natural Ban in Argentina. Soon after purchasing Argentina's previously government-owned natural gas company, Gas Natural, a Spanish-owned company, launched a Gas for All campaign aimed at delivering cheap natural gas to squatter settlements in Buenos Aires and thus eliminating the need for residents to purchase more costly propane in tanks. The dilemma was that although natural gas delivered to homes was cheaper than the canned gas residents were purchasing on their own, the absence of transmission pipes in the squatter neighborhoods left the poor out of the system, but the residents could not afford the prices the company would have to charge to cover the cost of laying the pipes. To solve this dilemma, the company worked out a financing arrangement with a government agency and then forged a partnership with a local nonprofit organization, Fundación Pro Vivienda Social (Foundation for Social Housing), to organize poor neighborhoods to support the extension of gas pipelines, to recruit and train community residents to perform the installation, and to train people to use natural gas and to manage their finances to avoid falling behind on their bills. Ultimately, thirty-five hundred dwellings were hooked up to natural gas through this initiative, saving the households' money while allowing the company to earn at least a modest profit.[23]

Other such bottom-of-the-pyramid product development and marketing experiments are also percolating in the region. Examples here include the following:

- The micro-credit program inaugurated by ABN AMRO Real Bank in Brazil to bring its financial experience to the task of promoting micro-enterprise development;
- The initiative launched by Colcerámica, a division of Colombia's Corona home materials company, to sell small quantities of ceramic tiles in low-income neighborhoods. A special feature of this initiative is Colcerámica's decision to recruit a local development association to recruit and train indigenous residents to market the tiles, and to allocate 3 percent of the proceeds of the sales to the development association and 7 percent to the entrepreneur-salespersons.[24]
- The partnership forged in Mexico between Bimbo, Mexico's huge multinational baking-goods company, and FinComún, a leading community-based financial institution formed in 1994 to provide access to credit for low-income micro-entrepreneurs in the region.[25] Bimbo has long operated in a

bottom-of-the-pyramid fashion, distributing its products not only through huge retail outlets but also through micro outlets in the remotest areas of the country. In Mexico City, with a population of more than eighteen million, there are said to be twice as many Bimbo delivery trucks as city police cars. But many of these micro outlets had difficulty paying in advance for the products, forcing Bimbo to organize a credit system, something it was not really equipped to do. The partnership with FinComún is designed to take advantage of FinComún's superior experience in extending credit to micro-enterprises. Under the partnership, FinComún loan advisers accompany Bimbo delivery drivers on their daily routes and have an opportunity to be introduced to the store owners and to make a brief presentation on FinComún and its services. In this way Bimbo hopes to sustain the delivery network so crucial to its bottom-of-the-pyramid marketing while strengthening an important community development institution.

Conclusion

Intriguing signs are thus in evidence that social engagement is not only influencing business external activities but also penetrating core business operations. Through changes in production processes, active supply-chain management, and social product development, as well as the incorporation of social responsibility activities into firm human-resources programs, companies are using their businesses, and not just their philanthropy, to advance their social engagement goals.

To be sure, there are risks in this course of action. Through this approach companies potentially make themselves vulnerable to charges that they are making profits on the poor. But the opposite risks are probably greater: that companies could appear to be disingenuous if they undercut, or even simply fail to address, in their business practices problems they claim to be trying to solve through their external social engagement activities. The penetration strategy brings the internal and external behavior into greater harmony and thus represents perhaps the highest form of social engagement.

While there is ample evidence that companies in the region are moving in this direction, the evidence is still anecdotal and inexact. Like other aspects of business social engagement, enormous variation exists from company to company and place to place. Yet there are enough outspoken advocates of this approach to have some hope that it, too, will continue to grow.

Chapter 7

Conclusion

Corporate social responsibility is best understood as a niche rather than a generic strategy: it makes business sense for some firms in some areas under some circumstances.
—DAVID VOGEL[1]

We need to stop thinking of our firms as business enterprises and begin thinking of them as social transformation agencies.
—GUILHERME PEIRÃO LEAL,
CEO, NATURA, BRAZIL

The new alliance for progress launched at the Cartagena conference in 1995 in an effort to mobilize greater business involvement in the task of alleviating poverty and protecting the environment in Latin America has now evolved into a raging movement with its own press, academic centers, diffusion agents, conferences, consultants, awards, lexicon, acronyms, heroes, and gurus.

A good part of the activity, no doubt, is pure public relations intended to improve the public image of the business sector and the market position of individual firms. What is more, the recent flurry of activity, while impressive, is hardly new. It rests upon a long—if far more personalistic and diffuse—tradition among at least some of the region's leading business families to "give something back," a tradition that often had its roots in deeply felt religious convictions.

But there is also evidence in the record reported here of a more widespread and strategic form of business social engagement

103

taking root in this region. Companies have thus moved extensively along the three key dimensions of the corporate social engagement pyramid that correspond most closely to the recommended MBA approach to this topic. Thus, corporate social engagement has *proliferated,* indeed exploded, touching wider segments of the business community in all five of the countries examined, though with considerable variations from place to place and industry to industry. Beyond this, the activity has become more *professionalized.* Identifiable institutional structures have been established, dedicated staff assigned, training provided, and efforts to forge coherent strategies undertaken. Indeed, a virtual CSR industry has emerged, consisting of professional diffusion agents, consultants, and assessment instruments that keep the topic on companies' radar screens and establish a competitive environment for business performance in this sphere. Finally, companies are beginning to engage basic problems and come to terms with the resulting need for longer time horizons and strategic *partnering* in order to gain meaningful traction on them. In all of these respects what is particularly notable is the sheer speed with which the corporate social engagement mantra has penetrated the region, at least in rhetoric if not yet fully in practice. This is doubtless due in important part to the role that the press has been willing to play in popularizing the concept, itself a form of social engagement on the part of the Latin press.

But more sets Latin American corporate social engagement apart than the speed and extent to which it has embraced the key features of the prevailing MBA approach. Perhaps even more notable is the extent to which corporations are pushing beyond this approach into the upper two reaches of what I earlier termed the corporate social engagement pyramid. As we have seen, this has involved, first, an emphasis on a consciously *participatory* approach to social engagement, in which companies actively reach out to disadvantaged communities and involve them in the design and operation of corporate engagement activities. This approach is evident in the work of the oil company Hocol in Colombia, of paper manufacturer Klabin in Brazil, and of the broader network of companies that have joined together in the RedEAmérica coalition forged by the IAF. Here corporate social engagement becomes a vehicle not only for providing temporary assistance, but also for achieving empowerment and self-reliance and thus overcoming the dependence and submissiveness that close observers have long found to be pervasive in Latin American society.

Equally striking is the evidence of *penetration* of corporate social engagement activity into core business functions—into production processes, supply-chain management, and basic product development and marketing. The work of Masisa in Chile; Natura, ABN-Amro Real Bank, and Wal-Mart in Brazil; Gas Natural Ban in Argentina; and Colcerámica in Colombia are just a few of the notable examples of this significant development. Indeed, at least some businesses are coming to see their firms as social transformation agents, uniquely positioned to produce the changes needed to put Latin American society on a path to sustained growth and social peace.

In none of these dimensions, however, is the progress in the region complete, or even nearly so, as the discussion here has also made clear. Not all companies have bought into the corporate social engagement concept. Fewer still have adopted a truly professional and strategic approach. While partnering has increased, civil society groups have often been left out of them, or brought in as junior partners at best. Participatory approaches are numerous but by no means the dominant mode of corporate interaction with communities. And penetration, while growing, is still somewhat of a fringe concept advanced by a small group of visionaries but implemented by only a handful of forward-thinking firms.

What is more, the progress achieved to date, in addition to being partial, is also far from permanent. The future of the trend-setting social engagement achievements of Brazil's ABN-Amro Real Bank have recently been called into question, for example, by the sale of the bank's parent company, the Dutch banking conglomerate ABN-Amro, to the Royal Bank of Scotland, and that bank itself has been severely shaken by the global credit crisis that began in 2007. The Human Resources staff of Alpina in Colombia had no sooner completed an ambitious redesign of its corporate social engagement strategy than new leadership dismissed the designers and set off in a different direction. On top of this, the global economic recession that struck in late 2007 and is continuing into 2010 has put corporate social engagement everywhere under severe pressure. Corporate social engagement officers therefore stand on all too shaky ground as shifts in leadership, reorganizations, and changing business conditions alter the environment in which they work, often with little warning.

Finally, there is some evidence that the variations in corporate social engagement experience that we have uncovered are far from random, that they reflect something far deeper than the attitudes of particular corporate leaders or the persuasiveness of the region's impressive corporate engagement diffusion agents. As David Vogel has argued in a recent book, "The supply of corporate virtue is both made possible and constrained by the market." What this means in practice is that corporate social engagement can be expected to flourish where market conditions make it especially necessary or useful and to languish where these conditions do not support it. Instead of seeing in the rise of Latin CSR a tidal shift that is converting Latin businesses into "social transformation agents," Vogel's argument suggests we should view it instead as merely a "niche" phenomenon that "makes business sense for some firms in some areas under some circumstances."[2]

This view certainly finds some support in the evidence reviewed here. Some of the most impressive advances in corporate social engagement in the region, after all, have come among the companies with the heaviest social and environmental impacts, such as the extractive oil and mineral industries in Colombia and Chile, and the paper and timber industries in Brazil. These firms require social peace in order to operate, and corporate social engagement, particularly corporate engagement with a participatory component, has increasingly proved to be one of the surest, and perhaps only, ways to secure it. Similarly, Wal-Mart Brazil's embrace of the *penetration* strategy was simply a particularly inventive response to what was essentially a basic business challenge—how to secure a reliable supply of high-quality products at competitive prices in an economy of sub-marginal producers. At times this niche quality of corporate social engagement even wears a personal face, as in the case of Banamex's decision to undertake a major community development and empowerment effort in Aqua Blanca and thirty other marginal communities in the far-off Ixmiquilpan area of Northern Mexico, in considerable part as a result of the personal brush with urban violence experienced by Banamex's president, Alfredo Harp.

More generally, the speed with which Latin American businesses have embraced corporate social engagement in recent years may have as much to do with the violent conditions in significant parts of the region, the strength of left-wing politics, and the election of Hugo Chávez as it does with the persuasiveness and tactical genius of the region's corporate social engagement advocates or some resulting philosophical shift in the mindset of Latin American corporate leaders. Time and again, as we have seen, corporate leaders pointed to the prevailing social and political realities of the region as principal impulses for the attention they are giving to social engagement, using dramatic images of a "fire around us" and a "time bomb" to convey the seriousness of the pressures helping to impel their interest in social engagement activities.

The key question this raises, of course, is whether the prevailing trend of growing commitment to corporate social engagement recorded here will survive an improvement in the general Latin American social and political situation, should such an improvement occur. In other words, does serious corporate social engagement in the region represent a permanent transformation or a passing fad? Is this a niche phenomenon in both time and space or a more fundamental and permanent transformation of the business system? Is the current surge of corporate social engagement doomed to repeat the sad history of the last great experiment in looking to "humane corporations" as "the chief instrument of social progress," the "welfare capitalism" movement in late nineteenth and early twentieth century United States? Ultimately, that movement turned out to be what its leading historian has termed a "temporary expedient, an interim solution [to the problems of industrialization]" that gained traction mainly as a response to labor organizing but petered out once the labor unrest subsided.[3]

One test of what the future holds for Latin corporate social engagement can be found in the record of how such engagement fared during the economic downturn after 2007. Unfortunately, that record is far from clear, but the impressions of close observers provide some basis for cautious optimism.[4] To be sure, the rapid proliferation of corporate social engagement that characterized the period leading up to this crisis has been suspended or seriously slowed in most of the countries on which we have information, and may have been at least partially reversed, at least among the small- and medium-sized firms. This has had a significant impact on the nonprofit organizations that rely on corporate contributions, particularly the small- and medium-sized ones that are not even able to offer the corporations visibility or public-relations impact in exchange for the donations they receive.[5]

But there is little evidence of wholesale suspension of corporate social engagement activity. To the contrary, at least along some dimensions of our corporate social engagement pyramid, there has been continuing progress. This has especially been true of the professionalization dimension. Faced with restricted resources, corporations have apparently responded by tightening their strategic focus. As Azócar has put it: "The crisis may be construed as the acid test that dislodges projects considered to be non-strategic by the enterprise and as a result reinforces the focus on the strategic ones."[6] Certainly there has been no reduction in enrollments in the region's numerous programs training corporate social engagement professionals.[7] Also notable has been the further penetration of corporate social engagement into the business practices of corporations and a growing business effort to engage the communities with which their operations interact. One sign of this is the continued expansion of companies issuing sustainability reports that document such penetration.

How can we explain such persistent commitment to corporate social engagement in the face of a withering economic crisis? From the evidence at hand, several factors seem to be at work. For one thing, companies seem to have bought into the notion that social engagement offers them competitive advantages, so much so that they are increasingly treating their social engagement activities as trade secrets.[8] Equally important is the fact that Latin American companies are increasingly competing on a global level, and corporate social engagement has grown increasingly salient among overseas consumers, especially in Europe. Exports have come to represent 25 percent of gross domestic product (GDP) in Colombia, for example, up from 10 percent in 1990.[9] This has substantially broadened the range of companies with an economic interest in bringing social and environmental concerns into their business operations. Finally, the economic crisis has further shaken public confidence in the business sector, leading to increased pressures from citizens and governments for greater corporate engagement in social and environmental problem solving. In Colombia, for example, the National Planning Department has sought to rally companies to participate in income-generation programs aimed at underprivileged populations and brought CSR requirements into its National Competitiveness Policy. In Chile, also, new environmental regulations require enterprises intending to undertake major projects to identify and find ways to resolve the environmental and social impacts of the projects and to incorporate meaningful citizen participation processes as they do so.

What this experience suggests is that there are significant forces sustaining and extending the corporate social engagement movement in the Latin American region. If corporate social engagement is a "niche" phenomenon, as Vogel suggests, that niche has grown quite broad in the Latin American context. At the same time, the future of this movement may depend as much on the social, political, and economic environment that businesses face as it does on the skills and knowledge of the business community itself. What this means in practice is that the promotion and strengthening of business social engagement cannot be achieved by initiatives aimed at the business community alone, important though these may be. Effort must also be put on strengthening what corporate accountability expert Simon Zadek has termed "the civil regulation of corporations,"[10] the social forces and organizations that will ultimately determine whether such engagement continues to be necessary for business survival and success. Included here are such things as consumer demand for responsible products, the presence of nonprofit organizations capable of monitoring corporate behavior and publicizing improprieties, actual or threatened boycotts of environmentally or socially exploitative firms, socially responsible investors willing to use their economic power to enforce good corporate practice, as well as business managers and employees inculcated with the values of corporate responsibility.[11]

There are two messages here for anyone interested in extending the "new alliance for progress" that has brought the Latin American business community into the effort to overcome poverty, deprivation, and environmental degradation in contemporary Latin America. The first is that this effort must be considerably extended if it is ultimately to succeed. Conferences, training seminars, networking events, award programs, best-practices case studies, and university courses targeted on the business community alone, while useful and necessary, are not sufficient. Significant effort must also be directed to the other social actors whose involvement will be necessary to keep the corporate sector focused on this aspect of its responsibility. This means training nonprofit leaders, supporting corporate watch-dog bodies, educating consumers, encouraging socially responsible investing by individuals and institutions, and promoting networking activities that bring corporate leaders together with their counterparts in the nonprofit and socially responsible investor communities.

The second message, however, is that such efforts are highly worthwhile. For all its limitations, the corporate social engagement movement in Latin America has generated enormous energy and produced some highly useful results. Aside from the individual program accomplishments, this movement has established a set of expectations that is already penetrating the corporate establishment and the public at large. More than that, it has fostered the creation of institutional structures both within individual businesses and among them that give considerable permanence to the effort. Finally, the Latin business community has founds ways to extend the corporate social engagement concept well beyond its MBA roots, establishing in the process its own distinctive Latin style and a corresponding sense of discovery and pride.

In short, while hardly all that some might hope for, there is enough substance to the Latin American corporate social engagement phenomenon to justify cautious optimism and to encourage expanded, though carefully focused, support.

Notes

1. Introduction:
A New Alliance for Progress?

1. Guilherme Peirão Leal (co-president, Natura), presentation to the Inter-American Development Bank's Inter-American Conference on Corporate Social Responsibility, Salvador, Brazil, December 10, 2006.

2. Francisco Aylwin Oyarzún, interview, May 2, 2006.

3. Cynthia Sanborn and Felipe Portocarrero, "Editor's Introduction," in *Philanthropy and Social Change in Latin America,* ed. Cynthia Sanborn and Felipe Portocarrero (Cambridge, MA: David Rockefeller Center Series on Latin American Studies, Harvard University, 2005), xi.

4. Jorge Gutiérrez, interview, November 8, 2006.

5. The term *social enterprise* is used in a wide variety of ways to refer to essentially nonprofit organizations that utilize the market to promote social objectives. See, for example, Jacques Defourny and Marthe Nyssens, "Defining Social Enterprise," *Social Enterprise: At the Crossroads of Market, Public Policies, and Civil Society,* ed. Marthe Nyssens (London: Routledge, 2006), 3–26.

6. Sanborn and Portocarrero, "Editor's Introduction," xi.

7. Michael E. Porter and Mark R. Kramer, "The Competitive Advantage of Corporate Philanthropy, " *Harvard Business Review* (December 2002): 5.

8. Antonio Vives and Estrella Peinado-Vara, "Introduction: Deeds Not Words," in *Corporate Social Responsibility: Deeds Not Words: Proceedings: II Inter-American Conference on Corporate Social Responsibility,* Mexico City, September 26–28, 2003, ed. Antonio Vives and Estrella Peinado-Vara (Washington DC: Inter-American Development Bank, 2004), 1.

9. Ibid.

10. "The Rich under Attack," *The Economist* (April 2, 2009).

11. As Cynthia Sanborn, an expert on Latin American philanthropy, has noted: "Few reliable estimates exist of the actual amount of private donations made in a given country and year, or of the magnitude of resources invested in philanthropic programs, nor do we have baseline data that allows us to confirm whether donations of various sorts have increased or decreased over time" (Cynthia Sanborn, "Philanthropy in Latin America: Historical Traditions and Current Trends," in Sanborn and Portocarrero, *Philanthropy and Social Change in Latin America*, 9).

12. The literature on corporate social responsibility has grown massively in recent years. One recent search on Google found thirty thousand sites for "corporate social responsibility," fifteen million pages of the World Wide Web devoted to it, and six hundred books on the topic listed by Google (David Vogel, *The Market for Virtue: The Potential and Limits of Corporate Social Responsibility,* Washington DC: Brookings Institution Press, 2005), 6. While many corporate reports exist on the Latin American component of this field, serious analyses of it are quite limited. No attempt has been made here, therefore, to offer a general assessment of this field. At the same time, well over one hundred books, articles, and reports on the topic and on Latin American social, economic, and political trends were examined as part of this work. I am indebted to Bernard Brown for assistance in identifying, accessing, and reviewing this literature. The bibliography provides a list of works consulted.

13. I am indebted to Gabriel Berger of Argentina, Marcos Kisil of Brazil, Ignacio Irrarázaval of Chile, Roberto Gutiérrez of Colombia, and Klaus German and Emilio Guerra Díaz of Mexico for their assistance in compiling these reports.

14. Bernard Brown and Alice Lariu were especially helpful in reviewing IAF grant records. Appreciation is also owed to IAF staff for assistance in gaining access to these records.

15. I am grateful to Jens Prinzhorn for his assistance in conducting these mini–case studies. Interviews conducted by Mr. Prinzhorn are identified as such. All other interviews cited were conducted by the author.

16. The *Proceedings* of the IDB's II Inter-American Conference on Corporate Social Responsibility, for example, defines CSR as "a business strategy that seeks to avoid causing damage to stakeholders through its activities, and wherever possible to bring them benefits, irrespective of whether the damage or benefits are subjects to legislation or regulation." Ronald Sims defines corporate social responsibility as a corporation's "obligation to engage in activities that protect or contribute to the welfare of society." The World Business Council for Sustainable Development (WBCSD) extends the concept further to embrace the notion of sustainable development. According to the WBCSD, "Corporate social responsibility is the commitment of business to sustainable economic development, working with employees, their families, the local community and society at large to improve their quality of life." See Vives and Peinado-Vara, "Introduction: Deeds Not Words," 2; Ronald Sims, *Ethics and Corporate Social Responsibility* (New York: Praeger, 2003), 44; World Business Council for Sustainable Development, *Corporate Social Responsibility: Making Good Business Sense* (Conches-Geneva, Switzerland: WBCSD, 2000), 11.

17. Instituto Ethos, *Ethos Corporate Social Responsibility Indicators* (São Paolo: Instituto Ethos, 2003).

18. For a useful discussion of the numerous ambiguities inherent in the corporate social engagement concept, see Vogel, *The Market for Virtue,* 4–6.

19. *The Economist,* "How Good Should Your Business Be?" (January 19, 2008): 12–13.

20. Craig Smith, "The New Corporate Philanthropy," *Harvard Business Review* 72, no. 1 (May/June 1994): 105–16; Reynold Levy, *Give and Take: A Candid Account of Corporate Philanthropy* (Cambridge, MA: Harvard Business School Press, 1999); Vogel, *The Market for Virtue*, 16; Porter and Kramer, "The Competitive Advantage of Corporate Philanthropy"; Michael E. Porter and Mark R. Kramer, "Strategy and Society: The Link between Competitive Advantage and Corporate Social Responsibility," *Harvard Business Review* (December 2006), 78–93; Noel M. Tichy, Andrew R. McGill, and Lynda St. Clair, eds., *Corporate Global Citizenship: Doing Business in the Public Eye* (San Francisco: The New Lexington Press, 1997).

21. Vogel, *The Market for Virtue*.

22. *The Economist*, "How Good Should Your Business Be?" 8.

23. Levy, *Give and Take*, 3–13.

24. Smith, "The New Corporate Philanthropy"; Porter and Kramer, "The Competitive Advantage of Corporate Philanthropy"; Porter and Kramer, "Strategy and Society."

25. Sanborn, "Philanthropy in Latin America," 7.

26. Francisco Durand, *Incertidumbre y Soledad. Reflexiones Sobre los Grandes Empresarios de America Latina* [*Uncertainty and solitude, reflections on the big business people of Latin America*] (Lima: Fundación Friedrich Ebert, 1996), 178.

27. *The Economist*, "How Good Should Your Business Be?" 13.

28. Sergio Haddad, interview, December 15, 2006.

29. Porter and Kramer, "Strategy and Society," 6.

30. Porter and Kramer, "The Competitive Advantage of Corporate Philanthropy," 9.

31. James Austin, *The Collaboration Challenge: How Nonprofits and Businesses Succeed through Strategic Alliances* (San Francisco: Jossey-Bass, 2000), 1–19. James Austin and Associates, *Social Partnering in Latin America: Lessons Drawn from Collaborations of Businesses and Civil Society Organizations* (Cambridge, MA: David Rockefeller Center for Latin American Studies, Harvard University, 2004), 29–42; Marion Ritchey-Vance, *The Art of Association: NGOs and Civil Society in Colombia* (Arlington, VA: Inter-American Foundation, 1991).

32. Sergio Haddad, interview, December 15, 2006.

33. Vogel, *The Market for Virtue*, 166.

34. Ibid., 17, 3. Opinions differ over why this is so. Vogel points to limitations imposed by the market, for example, consumer disinterest, the limited scale of socially oriented investment compared to other investment, and the other factors impinging on worker decisions about where to work (ibid. 3, 46, 25, 57, 59). Others point to limitations in the application of the MBA paradigm. Porter and Kramer, for example, argue that this paradigm is simply not being implemented effectively, that "what passes for 'strategic philanthropy' today is almost never truly strategic, and often isn't even particularly effective as philanthropy. . . . The majority of corporate contributions programs are diffuse and unfocused" (Porter and Kramer, "The Competitive Advantage of Corporate Philanthropy," 5). Returning to the

topic four years later Porter and Kramer found little evidence of improvement, noting that "the prevailing approaches to CSR are so fragmented and so disconnected from business and strategy as to obscure many of the greatest opportunities for companies to benefit society" (Porter and Kramer, "Strategy and Society," 2).

35. The depiction of traditional business philanthropy in Latin America here draws heavily on the following sources: Sanborn, "Philanthropy in Latin America," 2005; Cristina Rojas and Gustavo Morales, "Private Contributions to the Public Sphere," in Sanborn and Portocarrero, *Philanthropy and Social Change in Latin America*; Mario M. Roitter and M. Camerlo, "Corporate Social Action in a Context of Crisis: Reflections on the Argentine Case," in Sanborn and Portocarrero, *Philanthropy and Social Change in Latin America*; Durand, *Incertidumbre y Soledad*; Bryan W. Hustad and Carlos Serrano, "Corporate Governance in Mexico," *Journal of Business Ethics* 37 (May 2002): 337–48. Available at www.kluweronline.com. Chapter 2 develops this portrait more fully.

36. Vogel, *The Market for Virtue*, 2–3.

2. Proliferation:
The Spread of Corporate Social Engagement

1. Jorge Villalobos, interview, May 9, 2005; Martha Del Rio Grimm, interview, October 18, 2005.

2. Felipe Agüero, "Promotion of Corporate Social Responsibility in Latin America," in Sanborn and Portocarrero, *Philanthropy and Social Change in Latin America*, 125.

3. IAF, Grant Files, 2007.

4. Luis Fernando Cruz, "La Experiencia de la Fundación Carvajal en el Desarrollo Social de Cali" [the experience of Fundación Carvajal in Cali's social development], in *Empresa Privada y Responsabilidad Social*, ed. Olga Lucia Toro and German Rey, 258–63 (Bogotá: Utopica Ediciones, 1996); IAF Grant Files, 2007.

5. IPEA, *A Iniciativa Privada e o Espírito Público: A evolução da ação social das empresas privadas no Brasil* (Brasilia: IPEA, 2002). Available at www.ipea.gov.br. The U.S. figure was computed from data in *Giving USA 2005* (Indianapolis: Giving USA Foundation, 2005).

6. IPEA, *A Iniciativa Privada e o Espírito Público: A evolução da ação social das empresas privadas no Brasil* (Brasilia: IPEA, 2006).

7. Oded Grajew, interview, Salvador, Brazil, December 6, 2006; Oded Grajew and Ricardo Young, "Manifesto for Sustainable Development," Instituto Ethos (2006).

8. Gabriel Berger, *Encuesta de Responsabilidad Social empresarial en Argentina—Ano 2005*, final report (Buenos Aires: UDESA/Gallup, 2005).

9. Gabriel Berger, *The New Alliance for Progress: Patterns of Business Engagement in Latin America—The Case of Argentina*, unpublished report (2007).

10. Ibid.

11. Claudio Bruzzi-Boechat, Dom Cabral Foundation, presentation at the IDB corporate social responsibility conference, Salvador, Brazil, December 12, 2006.

12. Ignacio Irrarázaval, interview, May 5, 2006.

13. Emilio Guerra Díaz, *IAF Corporate Social Engagement Project—Country Report: México,* unpublished report (2007).

14. IPEA, *A Iniciativa Privada e o Espírito Público* (2002); Ignacio Irrarázaval, *The New Alliance for Progress: Emerging Patterns of Business Social Engagement in Latin America—The Case of Chile,* unpublished report (2007); Berger, *Encuesta de Responsabilidad Social empresarial en Argentina—Ano 2005;* Gabriel Berger, *Estudio de Filantropía Empresaria* (Buenos Aires: UDESA/Gallup, 1998).

15. Istar Jimena Gómez, interview, November 9, 2006.

16. Juliana Andrigueto, interview by Jens Prinzhorn, June 12, 2007.

17. IAF Grant Files, 2007.

18. Jose Ojeda, interview, May 5, 2006.

19. Fernando Peón Escalante, interview, May 11, 2005.

20. Martha Eugenia Hernández, interview, October 17, 2005.

21. Grajew, interview, December 12, 2006.

22. Maria Bettina Llapur, interview, May 10, 2007.

23. Wilson Newton de Mello Neto, interview, December 7, 2006.

24. For further detail on these developments, see, for example, Leslie Elliott Armijo and Philippe Faucher, "'We Have a Consensus': Explaining Political Support for Market Reforms in Latin America," *Latin American Politics and Society* 44, no. 2 (2002); Ernest Bartell, "Perceptions by Business Leaders and the Transition to Democracy in Chile," in *Business and Democracy in Latin America,* ed. Ernest Bartell and Leigh A. Payne, 49–104 (Pittsburgh: University of Pittsburgh Press, 1995); Eduardo Silva, *The State and Capital in Chile: Business Elites, Technocrats, and Market Economics* (Boulder, CO: Westview Press, 1996); Manuel R. Agosin and Ernesto Pasten, "Corporate Governance in Chile," paper presented at the Policy Dialogue Meeting on Corporate Governance in Developing Countries and Emerging Economies, OECD Headquarters, Paris, Organization of Economic Co-operation and Development, OECD Development Centre, April 23–24, 2001. Available at www.oecd.org; Rabelo Coutinho, *Corporate Governance in Brazil* (Paris: Organization for Economic Co-operation and Development, 2001).

25. IPEA, www.ipea.gov.br, 2002, cited in Marcos Kisil, "Corporate Social Engagement and Corporate-Civil Society Partnership in Brazil," unpublished report (2006).

26. Kisil, "Corporate Social Engagement and Corporate-Civil Society Partnership in Brazil."

27. Marcelo M. Giugale, Olivier Lafourcade, and Connie Luff, eds., *Colombia: The Economic Foundation of Peace* (Washington DC: The World Bank, 2003); Elsie Garsfield and Jairo Arboleda, "Violence, Sustainable Peace, and Development," in ibid.

28. Instituto Ethos, *Perfil Social, Racial, e de Gênero dos Diretores de Grandes Empresas Brasileiras [Social, racial, and gender profile of the directors of large*

Brazilian companies] (São Paulo: Instituto Ethos, January, 2002), 15. Available at www.ethos.org.br/.

29. Luis Norberto Paschoal, interview, December 13, 2006.

30. Grajew, interview, December 12, 2006.

31. Evelina Dagnino, "Os Movimentos Sociais e a emergência de uma Nova Cidadania," in *Anos 90: Política e Sociedade no Brasil,* ed. E. Dabnnino (São Paulo: Brasiliense, 1994), quoted in Kisil, "Corporate Social Engagement and Corporate-Civil Society Partnership in Brazil."

32. Lester M. Salamon, "The Rise of Nonprofit Organizations," *Foreign Affairs* 73, no. 4 (July/August, 1994); Julie Fisher, *The Road from Rio: Sustainable Development and the Nongovernmental Movement in the Third World* (Westport, CT: Praeger, 1993); Marion Ritchey-Vance, *The Art of Association: NGOs and Civil Society in Colombia* (Arlington, VA: IAF, 1991); Lester M. Salamon et al., *La Sociedad Civil Global* (Bilboa: Fundación BBVA, 1999), published in English as *Global Civil Society: Dimensions of the Nonprofit Sector* (Baltimore: Johns Hopkins Center for Civil Society Studies, 1999).

33. Silva, *The State and Capital in Chile,* 1996.

34. The account in this and subsequent paragraphs draws on personal interviews with Valdemar de Oliveira Neto, June 6, 2005; Grajew, interview, December 12, 2006; Marcos Kisil, December 14, 2006; Sérgio Mindlin, December 13, 2006; Ricardo Young, December 14, 2006.

35. Mario M. Roitter and M. Camerlo, "Corporate Social Action in a Context of Crisis: Reflections on the Argentine Case," in Sandborn and Portocarrero, *Philanthropy and Social Change in Latin America,* 229.

36. Daniel Chudnovsky, Bernardo Kosacoff, and Andres Lopez, *Las Multinacionales Latinoamericanas: Sus Estrategias en un Mundo Globalizado* [Latinamerican multinationals: Their strategies in a globalized world] (Buenos Aires: Fondo de Cultura Economica, 1999), 18, 29.

37. Rita De Cássia Guedes, "Responsabilidade Social y Cidadania Empresariais: Conceitos Estrategicos Para As Empresas Face a Globalização" [Corporate social responsibility and citizenship: Strategic concepts for businesses in globalization], Third Meeting of the Latin American and Caribbean Network of the ISTR, Buenos Aires, Argentina, September, 2001.

38. Francisco Durand, Incertidumbre y Soledad, Reflexiones Sobre los Grandes Empresarios de America Latina [Uncertainty and solitude, reflections on the big business people of Latin America] (Lima: Fundación Friedrich Ebert, 1996).

39. Agüero, "Promotion of Corporate Social Responsibility," 124.

40. Antonio Vives and Estrella Peinado-Vara, *Corporate Social Responsibility as a Tool for Competitiveness: Proceedings,* Inter-American Conference for Corporate Social Responsibility, Panama City, October 26–28, 2003 (Washington DC: IAD, 2004).

41. Luis Norberto Paschoal, interview, December 13, 2006.

42. Sérgio Mindlin, interview, December 13, 2006.

43. Active diffusion agents surfaced in the other countries considered here as well. In Chile, for example, Accion RSE and Pro-Humana have played similar roles (see their websites).

44. Cristina Carvalho Pinto, interview, December 14, 2006.

45. The discussion here draws on the following: Kisil, "Corporate Social Engagement"; Agüero, "Promotion of Corporate Social Responsibility"; and Grajew, interview, December 12, 2006; Marcello Linguette, interview, July 16, 2003; Paulo Itacarambi, interview, July 9, 2003; Mindlin, interview, December 13, 2006.

46. Instituto Ethos, *Ethos Indicators: Ethos Corporate Social Responsibility Indicators* (São Paulo: Instituto Ethos, 2003).

47. Mindlin, interview, December 13, 2006.

48. The discussion here is based on interactions with CEMEFI over a period of years; Villalobos, interview, May 9, 2005; Manuel Arango Arias, interview, October 17, 2005.

49. Berger, *The New Alliance for Progress*, 2007.

50. Irrarázaval, *The New Alliance for Progress—The Case of Chile*.

51. Roberto Gutiérrez, Iván Darío Lobo, and Diana M. Trujillo, "Corporate Social Engagement in Colombia," unpublished report (2007).

52. Alejandra Tironi Valdivieso, interview, May 4, 2006; Irrarázaval, *The New Alliance for Progress—The Case of Chile*.

53. Kisil, interviews, October 5, 2002, and December 14, 2006.

54. IAF, *Fiscal Year 1999 Active Grants Results Report* (Washington DC: IAF, 1999).

55. Walter Price, interview, August 3, 2005.

56. Based on a review of IAF grant records extending from 1995 to 2005.

57. Francisco Aylwin Oyarzún, interview, May 2, 2007.

58. Price, interview, August 3, 2005; Rodrigo Villar, interview, August 3, 2005; Sele Aguiar (Arcor Corporation), presentation at the IV Inter-American Development Bank Conference on CSR, Salvador, Brazil, December 11, 2006.

59. Silvio José Schlosser, interview, May 7, 2006.

60. Oyarzun, interview, May 2, 2006.

61. Roitter and Camerlo, "Corporate Social Action in a Context of Crisis," 235.

3. Professionalization

1. Claude Monnet, *Memoirs* (New York: Doubleday and Co., 1978), quoted in Reynold Levy, *Give and Take: A Candid Account of Corporate Philanthropy* (Cambridge: Harvard Business School Press, 1999), 107.

2. Constanza Gorleri, interview, May 8, 2007; Banco Galicia, *Informe de Responsibilidad Social Corporative 2005* (Buenos Aires: Banco Galicia, 2006).

3. See, for example, Antonio Vives and Estrella Peinado-Vara, *Corporate Social Responsibility as a Tool for Competitiveness: Proceedings*, Inter-American Conference for Corporate Social Responsibility, Panama City, October 26–28, 2003 (Washington DC: IDB, 2004); Antonio Vives and Estrella Peinado-Vara, "Introduction: Deeds Not Words," *Corporate Social Responsibility: Deeds Not Words: Proceedings*, II Inter-American Conference on Corporate Social

Responsibility, Mexico City, September 26–28, 2004 (Washington DC: Inter-American Development Bank, 2005); Craig Smith, "The New Corporate Philanthropy," *Harvard Business Review* (May 1994); Levy, *Give and Take*; Michael E. Porter and Mark R. Kramer, "The Competitive Advantage of Corporate Philanthropy," *Harvard Business Review* (December 2002): 5–16; Michael E. Porter and Mark R. Kramer, "Strategy and Society: The Link Between Competitive Advantage and Corporate Social Responsibility," *Harvard Business Review* (December 2006) 78–93; Mario M. Roitter and M. Camerlo, "Corporate Social Action in a Context of Crisis: Reflections on the Argentine Case," in Sanborn and Portocarrero, *Philanthropy and Social Change in Latin America*, 223–51.

4. Cristina Rojas and Gustavo Morales, "Private Contributions to the Public Sphere," in Sanborn and Portocarrero, *Philanthropy and Social Change in Latin America*, 166.

5. Ibid., 168.

6. This desire to institutionalize and professionalize corporate social engagement may also explain the stipulation of the Inter-American Foundation that participants in its RedEAmérica Network must be foundations, and not simply companies.

7. Gabriel Berger, *Encuesta de Responsabilidad Social empresarial en Argentina—Ano 2005,* final report (Buenos Aires: UDESA/Gallup, 2005), cited in Gabriel Berger, *The New Alliance for Progress: Patterns of Business Engagement in Latin America—The Case of Argentina,* unpublished report (2007).

8. Berger, *Encuesta de Responsabilidad Social empresarial en Argentina—Ano 2005*; Roitter and Camerlo, "Corporate Social Action in a Context of Crisis," 226–30.

9. Emilia Ruiz, interview, November 11, 2006; Roberto Gutiérrez, interview, November 7, 2006.

10. Carlos Romero and Angel Maas, "Bimbo Group and Papalote Museo del Niño," Social Enterprise Knowledge Network, SKE018, unpublished case study (July 25, 2003).

11. Luis Norberto Paschoal, interview, December 13, 2006.

12. Fernando Peón Escalante, interview, May 11, 2005.

13. Berger, *Encuesta de Responsabilidad Social empresarial en Argentina—Ano 2005*.

14. IPEA, *A Iniciativa Privada e o Espírito Público: A evolução da ação social das emresas privadas no Brasil* (Brasilia: IPEA, 2006).

15. Gabriel Altamirano Hernandez, interview, May 10, 2005.

16. Peón Escalante, interview, May 11, 2005.

17. Fernando Rosetti, interview, December 13, 2006; Maria Luiza de Oliveira Pinto, interview, December 13, 2006.

18. A substantial literature has emerged suggesting how this can best be done and how to square business objectives with societal needs in a way that produces shared value for both. See, for example, Vives and Peinado-Vara, *Corporate Social Responsibility as a Tool for Competitiveness*, 10–11; Smith, "The New Corporate Philanthropy"; Porter and Kramer, "The Competitive

Advantage of Corporate Philanthropy;" Porter and Kramer, "Strategy and Society."

19. Cynthia Sanborn, "Philanthropy in Latin America: Historical Traditions and Current Trends," in Sanborn and Portocarrero, *Philanthropy and Social Change in Latin America*, 4.

20. Rosetti, interview, December 13, 2006.

21. IPEA, *A Iniciativa Privada e o Espírito Público* (2006), as cited in Marcos Kisil, *Corporate Social Engagement and Corporate-Civil Society Partnership in Brazil*, unpublished report (2006).

22. Ignacio Irrarázaval, *The New Alliance for Progress: Emerging Patterns of Business Social Engagement in Latin America—The Case of Chile*, unpublished report (2007).

23. Berger, *Encuesta de Responsabilidad Social empresarial en Argentina—Ano 2005*; Sergio Haddad, interview, December 15, 2006.

24. Porter and Kramer, "The Competitive Advantage of Corporate Philanthropy"; Porter and Kramer, "Strategy and Society."

25. Rosa Maria Fischer, "Intersectoral Alliances and the Reduction of Social Exclusion," in Sanborn and Portocarrero, *Philanthropy and Social Change in Latin America*, 148; Berger, *Encuesta de Responsabilidad Social empresarial en Argentina—Ano 2005*; Irrarázaval, *The New Alliance for Progress—The Case of Chile*.

26. Silvio José Schlosser, interview, May 7, 2007.

27. Diego Sarmiento Gomez, interview, November 7, 2006.

28. Schlosser, interview, May 7, 2007; Sarmiento Gomez, interview, November 7, 2006.

29. De Oliveira Pinto, interview, December 13, 2006; Rosabeth Moss Kanter and Ricard Reisen de Pinho, *ABN-AMRO REAL: Banking on Sustainability* (Cambridge: Harvard Business School, October 2005).

30. Maria Del Pilar Bolivar Garcia, interview, November 9, 2006.

31. Wendy Arenas-Wightman, interview, November 10, 2006.

32. Sérgio Mindlin, interview, December 13, 2006.

33. Cited in Marcos Kisil, "Corporate Social Engagement and Corporate-Civil Society Partnership in Brazil," unpublished report (2006), 37; Berger, *Encuesta de Responsabilidad Social empresarial en Argentina—Ano 2005*.

34. Berger, *Encuesta de Responsabilidad Social empresarial en Argentina—Ano 2005*; Kisil, "Corporate Social Engagement and Corporate-Civil Society Partnership in Brazil."

35. Schlosser, interview, May 7, 2007.

36. De Oliveira Pinto, interview, December 13, 2006.

37. Juan Alberto Gonzalez Esparza, interview, November 7, 2006.

38. Carla Cordery Duprat, interview, December 14, 2006.

4. Partnering

1. Juan Pedro Pinochet (executive director, Un Techo para Chile [A roof for Chile]), quoted in Ignacio Irrarázaval, *The New Alliance for Progress:*

Emerging Patterns of Business Social Engagement in Latin America—The Case of Chile, unpublished report (2007).

2. Istar Jimena Gómez, interview, November 9, 2006; Mauricio Gómez, interview by Jens Prinzhorn, June 20, 2007.

3. James E. Austin, Ezequiel Reficco, and SEKN Research Team, "Building Cross-sector Bridges," in *Social Partnering in Latin America: Lessons Drawn from Collaborations of Businesses and Civil Society Organizations,* ed. James Austin and Associates, 42–71 (Cambridge, MA: David Rockefeller Center for Latin American Studies, Harvard University, 2004) .

4. Gabriel Berger. *Encuesta de Responsabilidad Social empresarial en Argentina—Ano 2005,* final report (Buenos Aires: UDESA/Gallup, 2005), cited in Gabriel Berger, *The New Alliance for Progress: Patterns of Business Engagement in Latin America—The Case of Argentina,* unpublished report (2007), 21.

5. IPEA, *A Iniciativa Privada e o Espírito Público: A evolução da ação social das emresas privadas no Brasil* (Brasilia: IPEA, 2006), cited in Marcos Kisil, "Corporate Social Engagement and Corporate-Civil Society Partnership in Brazil," unpublished report (2006); Irrarázaval, *The New Alliance for Progress—The Case of Chile,* 26.

6. Michael E. Porter and Mark R. Kramer, "The Competitive Advantage of Corporate Philanthropy," *Harvard Business Review* (December 2002), 9.

7. Berger, *Encuesta de Responsabilidad Social empresarial en Argentina—Ano 2005,* cited in Berger, *The New Alliance for Progress—The Case of Argentina,* 23.

8. IPEA, *A Iniciativa Privada e o Espírito Público,* 2006, cited in Kisil, "Corporate Social Engagement and Corporate-Civil Society Partnership in Brazil."

9. Beatriz Balian de Tagtachian, *Responsabilidad Social Empresaria: Un estudio empirico de 147 empresas,* series F, no. 1 (Buenos Aires: Universidad Católica Argentina, Facultad de Ciencias Económicas y Sociales, 2004), 15, cited in Berger, *The New Alliance for Progress—The Case of Argentina,* 24.

10. IPEA, *A Iniciativa Privada e o Espírito Público,* cited in Kisil, "Corporate Social Engagement and Corporate-Civil Society Partnership in Brazil."

11. Austin, Reficco, and SEKN Research Team, "The Key Collaboration Questions," 20–48, and "Concluding Reflections," 336, in Austin and Associates, *Social Partnering in Latin America.*

12. Rosa Maria Fischer, "Intersectoral Alliances and the Reduction of Social Exclusion," in *Philanthropy and Social Change in Latin America,* ed. Cynthia Sanborn and Felipe Portocarrero (Cambridge, MA: The David Rockefeller Center on Latin American Studies, Harvard University, 2005), 150

13. Sergio Mindlin, interview, December 13, 2006.

14. Alvaro Trespalacios Peñas, interview, November 9, 2006; Camilo Bernal Hadad, interview, November 10, 2006.

15. Susana Rojas-González de Castilla, interview, October 20, 2005; Francisco Aylwin Oyarzún, interview, May 2, 2006.

16. Balian de Tagtachian, *Responsabilidad Social Empresaria,* 17, cited in Berger, *The New Alliance for Progress—The Case of Argentina,* 25.

17. Austin, Reficco, and SEKN Research Team, "The Key Collaboration Questions," 17.

18. Roberto Gutiérrez, interview, November 7, 2006; Sergio Haddad, interview, December 15, 2006.

19. Alwyn Oyarzún, interview, May 2, 2006; León Guzmán Gatica, interview by Jens Prinzhorn, May 3, 2006; Emilia Ruiz, interview, November 11, 2006; Cynthia Sanborn, "Philanthropy in Latin America: Historical Traditions and Current Trends," in Sanborn and Portocarrero, *Philanthropy and Social Change in Latin America*, 22.

20. Haddad, interview, December 15, 2006; Guzman Gatica, interview, May 3, 2006; Manuel Arias Arango, interview, Mexico, October 17, 2005; Fischer, "Intersectoral Alliances and the Reduction of Social Exclusion," 159; Emilio Guerra Díaz, *IAF Corporate Social Engagement Project—Country Report: México*, unpublished report (2006), 26. On the historic Latin American suspicion of the entrepreneurial class, see Rabelo Coutinho, *Corporate Governance in Brazil* (Paris: Organization for Economic Cooperation and Development, 2001), 39; Francisco Durand, *Incertidumbre y Soledad. Reflexiones Sobre los Grandes Empresarios de America Latina* [*Uncertainty and solitude: Reflections on the big business people of Latin America*] (Lima: Fundación Friedrich Ebert, 1996).

21. Aylwin Orazún, interview, May 2, 2006; IPEA, *A Iniciativa Privada e o Espírito Público*, cited in Kisil, "Corporate Social Engagement and Corporate-Civil Society Partnership in Brazil"; Díaz, *IAF Corporate Social Engagement Project—Country Report: México,* 27. The Merced Foundation in Mexico operates CSR programs for various companies in Mexico (for example, Philip Morris, Nike, and Citigroup). As part of its program, it operates a "Strength" program to improve CSO institutional capacity, and a "Certainty" program to certify civic associations as worthy partners of foundations.

22. Agüero refers to this phenomenon as the "normative idea of the *empresa*" (see Felipe Agüero, "Promotion of Corporate Social Responsibility in Latin America," in Sanborn and Portocarrero, *Philanthropy and Social Change in Latin America*, 125).

23. On the "welfare capitalism" movement in the United States, see Stuart D. Brandes, *American Welfare Capitalism, 1880–1940* (Chicago: University of Chicago Press, 1976), 10–28, 148.

24. Bernardo Toro, interview, November 10, 2006; Wendy Arenas-Wightman, interview, November 10, 2006.

25. James Austin, *The Collaboration Challenge: How Nonprofits and Businesses Succeed through Strategic Alliances* (San Francisco: Jossey-Bass, 2000), 41.

26. Ciro Fleury, interview, December 15, 2006.

5. Participation

1. The discussion of the Hocol approach in this chapter draws on the following interviews: Ramiro Santa, November 10, 2006; Karen Ausderau, interview by Jens Prinzhorn, June 21, 2007; Juan Manuel Cuéllar Cabrera, interview by Jens Prinzhorn, June 21, 2007; Betty Marlena Páez Guitiérrez, interview by Jens Prinzhorn, June 22, 2007; Nury Cabrera, interview by Jens Prinzhorn, June 22, 2007; Salvador Dussan Medina, interview by Jens

Prinzhorn, June 22, 2007; Vianney Cabrera, interview by Jens Prinzhorn, June 22, 2007; Consuelo Forero, interview by Jens Prinzhorn, June 22, 2006.

2. Ramiro Santa, interview, November 10, 2006.

3. Evelina Dagnino, "Os Movimentos Sociais e a emergência de uma Nova Cidadania," in *Anos 90: Política e Sociedade no Brasil,* ed. E. Dabnnino (São Paulo: Brasiliense, 1994), quoted in Marcos Kisil, "Social Engagement and Corporate-Civil Society Partnership in Brazil," unpublished report (2006).

4. John P. Lewis, "Strengthening the Poor: Some Lessons for the International Community," in *Strengthening the Poor: What Have We Learned?* ed. John P. Lewis (New Brunswick: Transaction Books, 1987), 9. The discussion here and in the subsequent paragraph also draws heavily on Lester M. Salamon, "The Rise of Nonprofit Organizations," *Foreign Affairs* 73, no. 4 (July/August 1994): 111–24. Norman Uphoff, "Assisted Self-Reliance: Working with, Rather than for, the Poor," in Lewis, *Strengthening the Poor,* 47–60; Moeen A. Qureshi, "The World Bank and NGOs: New Approaches," paper delivered at the Washington chapter of the Society for International Development conference entitled "Learning from the Grassroots" (April 1988), 2; Aga Khan Foundation, "The Nairobi Statement," report of the Enabling Environment Conference: Effective Private Sector Contribution to Development in Sub-Sahara Africa, Nairobi, Kenya (Geneva: Aga Khan Foundation, 1987), 13; OECD, *The Welfare State in Crisis* (Paris: OECD, 1989), 77; UN, *Global Outlook 2000: An Economic, Social, and Environmental Perspective* (New York: UN, 1990), 8; Michael Cernea, "Farmer Organizations and Instituion Building for Sustainable Development," *Regional Development Dialogue* 8, no. 2 (Summer 1987): 1–19.

5. Hocol, *Sustainability Report 2005* (Bogotá, Colombia: Hocol, 2005).

6. Ramiro Santa, Interview, November 10, 2006.

7. Cristina Rojas and Gustavo Morales, "Private Contributions to the Public Sphere," in Sanborn and Portocarrero, *Philanthropy and Social Change in Latin America,* 174–75.

8. Bernardo Toro, interview, November 9, 2006.

9. For a discussion of the IAF's work, see Albert O. Hirschman, *Getting Ahead Collectively* (New York: Pergamon Press, 1984); and Marion Ritchey-Vance, *The Art of Association: NGOs and Civil Society in Colombia* (Arlington, VA: IAF, 1991).

10. The discussion in this paragraph and the ones directly following draw heavily on IAF internal files accessed with the assistance of Ms. Alice Lariu and interviews with the following: Steve Pierce, January 25, 1995; Walter Price, August 3, 2005; Linda Kolko, January 25, 2005, and Rodrigo Villar, August 3, 2005.

11. Silvana Comelli, interview, May 9, 2007; Claudio Giomi, interview, May 10, 2007; and Santos Lio, interview, May 10, 2007.

12. Emilia Ruiz, interview, November 11, 2006; Price, interview, August 3, 2005; Villar, interview, August 3, 2005.

13. Javier Moncayo, interview, November 7, 2006.

14. The discussion here is based on the following interviews: Wilberto Lima, Jr., interview, December 15, 2006; Marcos Kisil, interviews, December

12 and 14, 2006; Marcia Woods, interview by Jens Prinzhorn, June 18, 2007; Marlene Batista da Silva, interview by Jens Prinzhorn, June 18, 2007; Osvaldo Sarnoski, interview by Jens Prinzhorn, June 16, 2007; Ricardo Arcanjo, interview by Jens Prinzhorn, June 18, 2007; Maria da Graça Marson Cella, interview by Jens Prinzhorn, July 3, 2007; José Mauricio do Vale, interview by Jens Prinzhorn, June 16, 2007; and Dalton A. Heitkoiter de Melo, President, Klabin, interview by Jens Prinzhorn, June 16, 2007.

15. The discussion in this section is based on Olga Lucia Toro and Natalia Pineda-Londoño, "Philanthropy and Social Justice in the Andes: The Case of Hocol S.A. and Fundación Hocol," unpublished paper (June 2004), 35–37, and the interviews cited in note 1 above.

16. Hocol, "Postura Politica," cited by Toro and Pineda-Londoño, "Philanthropy and Social Justice." See also Hocol, *Sustainability Report 2005*, 5.

17. The discussion here draws on the following sources: Juliana Andrigueto, Presentation at IV Inter-American Conference on CSR, Salvador, Brazil, December 12, 2006; Juliana Andrigueto, interview, June 12, 2007; Gabriel Moraes, June 14, 2007; Edgar von Buettner, June 14, 2007; and community activists involved in the Barroso Project, June 15, 2007.

18. The discussion here is based on interviews with Fernando Peón Escalante, May 11, 2005; Hernan Ponce, October 20, 2005; Salvador Garcia Angulo, October 21, 2005; and a field visit to Aguas Blancas, October 20, 2005.

6. Penetration

1. Michael E. Porter and Mark R. Kramer, "The Competitive Advantage of Corporate Philanthropy," *Harvard Business Review* (December 2002): 5–16.

2. Maria Emilia Correa, interview, June 5, 2007.

3. Julio Moura, presentation at the Inter-American Development Bank VI Inter-American Conference on Corporate Social Responsibility, Salvador, Brazil, December 10, 2006. For information on the WBCSD, see www.wbcsd.org.

4. Ciro Fleury, interview, December 15, 2006.

5. Oded Grajew and Ricardo Young, "Manifesto for Sustainable Development," Instituto Ethos (2006); Oded Grajew, interview, December 12, 2006; Ricardo Young, interview, December 14, 2006; Paulo Itacarambi, interview, July 9, 2003.

6. Juan Alberto González Esparza, interview, November 7, 2006; Constanza Gorleri, interview, May 10, 2007.

7. ISO 26000 on CSR in general has now been prepared. On the ISO standards, see the iso.org website.

8. Manuel Arango Arias, interview, October 17, 2005.

9. The discussion here and in the immediately following paragraphs draws on Maria Luiza de Oliveira Pinto, interview, December 13, 2006; and Rosabeth Moss Kanter and Ricard Reisen de Pinho, *ABN-AMRO REAL:*

Banking on Sustainability (Cambridge: Harvard Business School, October 25, 2005).

10. The discussion of Masisa in this and subsequent paragraphs draws on María Emilia Correa, interview by Jens Prinzhorn, June 5, 2007; Ximena Abogabir, interview with Jens Prinzhorn, June 5, 2007; and GrupoNueva, *Annual Report* (2007).

11. Correa, interview by Jens Prinzhorn, June 5, 2007.

12. Wilberto Luíz Lima, interviews, December 15, 2006, and June 2, 2007; Klabin, *Relatório de Sustenabilidade* (São Paolo: Klabin, 2006); Jorge Siegrist Prado, interview, May 9, 2005; Costanza Gorleri, interview, May 8, 2007.

13. Berger, *The New Alliance for Progress: Patterns of Business Engagement in Latin America—The Case of Argentina,* unpublished report (2007); Costanza Gorleri, interview, May 10, 2009.

14. The discussion of the Wal-Mart case in this and subsequent paragraphs draws on Daniela de Fiori, interview by Jens Prinzhorn. June 13, 2007; Wilson de Mello Neto, presentation at V Inter-American Conference on Corporate Social Responsibility, Salvador, Brazil, December 12, 2007; Instituto Wal-Mart (2007); Wal-Mart Brazil, "Brazil Sustainability Strategy," Powerpoint Presentation, January 10, 2007; Artesanato Solidário (Artesol), *Quem Somos* (2007).

15. Artesanato Solidário (Artesol), *Quem somos.*

16. Marcos Kisil, "Corporate Social Engagement and Corporate-Civil Society Partnership in Brazil," unpublished report (2006), 53.

17. Maria Luiza de Oliveira Pinto, interview, December 13, 2006; Constanza Gorleri, interview, May 8, 2007; Claudio Giomi, May 10, 2007.

18. C. K. Pralahad, *The Fortune at the Bottom of the Pyramid: Eradicating Poverty through Profits* (Philadelphia: Wharton School Press, 2004).

19. Cristina Rojas and Gustavo Morales, "Private Contributions to the Public Sphere," in *Philanthropy and Social Change in Latin America,* ed. Cynthia Sanborn and Felipe Portocarrero (Cambridge, MA: David Rockefeller Center on Latin American Studies, Harvard University, 2005), 170.

20. Jorge Gutiérrez Sampedo, Colsubsidio, interview, Bogotá, November 8, 2006; Colsubsidio, *Informe y Balance General 2005* (Bogotá: Colsubsidio, 2006), 26–68.

21. Sutia Kim Alter, "Social Enterprise: A Typology of the Field Contextualized in Latin America," working paper (Washington DC: IDB, August 2003); *Foundation Carvajal: A Social Enterprise.* Available on the www.carvajal.com.co website.

22. James Austin, Ezequiel Reficco, and SEKN Research Team, *Social Partnering in Latin America: Lessons Drawn from Collaborations of Businesses and Civil Society Organizations* (Cambridge: David Rockefeller Center for Latin American Studies, Harvard University, 2004), 82–83.

23. Maria Bettina Llapur, interview, May 10, 2007.

24. Roberto Gutiérrez, interview, November 7, 2006.

25. David Grayson and Adrian Hodges, "Grupo Bimbo—Baking with Microfinance in Mexico," *Ethical Corporation* (December 14, 2006); Marta Eugenia Hernandez, interview, October 17, 2005.

7. Conclusion

1. David Vogel, *The Market for Virtue: The Potential and Limits of Corporate Social Responsibility* (Washington DC: Brookings Institution Press, 2005), 3.

2. Ibid.

3. Stuart D. Brandes, *American Welfare Capitalism, 1880–1940* (Chicago: University of Chicago Press, 1976), 10–28, 148.

4. The observations here are based on the following brief reports provided to the author: Javier Zulueta Azócar, "The Impact of the Crisis on Entrepreneurial Social Responsibility (ESR) in Chile," unpublished report (2009); Roberto Gutiérrez, "Forces at the Macro and Micro Levels: Colombia," unpublished report (2009); Marcos Kisil, "Update on CSR and the Economic Crisis: Brazil," unpublished report (2009).

5. Azócar, "Impact of the Crisis on Entrepreneurial Social Responsibility (ESR) in Chile," 3.

6. Ibid., 4.

7. Gabriel Berger, interview, August 10, 2009.

8. One informant reported that a company on which a case study was being prepared by university researchers requested that its name be withheld because it knew that its competitors were seeking information about its successful initiatives (Gutiérrez, "Forces at the Macro and Micro Levels: Colombia," 1).

9. Ibid.

10. Simon Zadek, cited in Vogel, *The Market for Virtue*, 3.

11. Vogel, *The Market for Virtue*, 3.

Bibliography

Every effort has been made to ensure that the URLs in this book are accurate and up to date. However, with the rapid changes that occur in the World Wide Web, it is inevitable that some pages or other resources will have been discontinued or moved, and some content modified or reorganized. The publisher recommends that readers who cannot find the sources or information they seek with the URLs in this book use one of the numerous search engines available on the Internet.

Books, Articles, Reports

Acuña, Carlos H. "Business Interests, Dictatorship, and Democracy in Argentina." In Bartell and Payne, *Business and Democracy in Latin America*, 3–48.

Aga Khan Foundation. "The Nairobi Statement." Report of the Enabling Environment Conference: Effective Private Sector Contribution to Development in Sub-Sahara Africa, Nairobi, Kenya. Geneva: Aga Khan Foundation, 1987.

Agosin, Manuel R., and Ernesto Pasten. "Corporate Governance in Chile." Paper presented at the Policy Dialogue Meeting on Corporate Governance in Developing Countries and Emerging Economies. Paris, OECD Development Centre, April 23–24, 2001. Available at www.oecd.org.

Agüero, Felipe. "Promotion of Corporate Social Responsibility in Latin America." In Sanborn and Portocarrero, *Philanthropy and Social Change in Latin America*, 103–34.

Alter, Sutia Kim. "Social Enterprise: A Typology of the Field Contextualized in Latin America." Working Paper. Washington DC: IDB, August 2003.

Arboleda, Jairo, and Elena Correa. "Forced Internal Displacement." In Giugale, Lafourcade, and Luff, *Colombia*, 825–48.

Armijo, Leslie Elliott, and Philippe Faucher. "'We Have a Consensus': Explaining Political Support for Market Reforms in Latin America." *Latin American Politics and Society* 44, no. 2 (2002): 1–41.

Artesanato Solidário (Artesol). *Quem somos*. Available at www.artesol.org.br/principal2.php.

Asocajas (Asociación Nacional de Cajas de Compensacion Familiar). *Responsibilidad Social del Sistema de Cajas de Compensación Familiar.* Bogotá: Asocajas, circa 2006.

Austin, James. *The Collaboration Challenge: How Nonprofits and Businesses Succeed through Strategic Alliances.* San Francisco: Jossey-Bass, 2000.

Austin, James, and Ezequiel Reficco. "Building Cross-sector Bridges," 29–74, "Concluding Reflections," 341–44, and "The Key Collaborations Questions," 23–28. In James Austin, Ezequiel Reficco, and Associates, *Social Partnering in Latin America: Lessons Drawn from Collaborations of Businesses and Civil Society Organizations,* 29–74. Cambridge, MA: David Rockefeller Center for Latin American Studies, Harvard University, 2004.

Azócar, Javier Zulueta. "The Impact of the Crisis on Entrepreneurial Social Responsibility (ESR) in Chile." Unpublished report, 2009.

Balian de Tagtachian, Beatriz. "Las Empresas y el Tercer Sector: Elementos Movilizadores y Obstaculizadores" [Businesses and the third sector: Mobilizing and restrictive elements]. Paper presented at the Second Meeting of the Latin American and Caribbean Network of ISTR, Santiago, Chile, September 1999.

———. *Responsabilidad Social Empresaria: Un estudio empirico de 147 empresas.* Series F, no. 1. Buenos Aires: Universidad Católica Argentina, Faculdad de Ciencias Económicas y Sociales, 2004.

Banco Galicia. *Informe de Responsabilidad Social Corporativa 2005.* Buenos Aires: Banco Galicia, 2006.

Barajas, Adolfo. "The Impact of Liberalization and Foreign Investment in Colombia's Financial Sector." *Journal of Development Economics* 63, no. 1 (October, 2000): 157–96.

Bartell, Ernest. "Perceptions by Business Leaders and the Transition to Democracy in Chile." In Bartell and Payne, *Business and Democracy in Latin America,* 49–104.

Bartell, Ernest, and Leigh A. Payne, eds. *Business and Democracy in Latin America.* Pittsburgh: University of Pittsburgh Press, 1995.

Bekerman, Marta, and Pablo Sirlin. "Static and Dynamic Impacts of Mercosur: The Case of the Footwear Sector." *CEPAL Review* 72 (December 2000): 179–95.

———. "Static and Dynamic Impacts of Mercosur: The Case of the Pharmaceutical Sector." *CEPAL Review* 75 (December 2001): 217–32.

Ber, M. *Coaliciones Empresariales con Fines Sociales. La Creación y el Funcionamiento de Alianzas de Responsabilidad Social entre Compañías.* Buenos Aires: Universidad de San Andrés, 2005.

Berger, Gabriel. *Encuesta de Responsabilidad Social empresarial en Argentina— Ano 2005.* Informe final. Buenos Aires: UDESA/Gallup, 2005.

———. *Estudio de Filantropía Empresaris.* Buenos Aires: UDESA/Gallup, 1998.

————. *The New Alliance for Progress: Patterns of Business Engagement in Latin America—The Case of Argentina*. Unpublished report, 2007.

Bonturi, Marcos. "Challenges in the Mexican Financial Sector." Economics Department Working Paper no. 339, OECD. August 23, 2002. Available at www.oecd.org.

Boron, Atilio A. "Becoming Democrats? Some Skeptical Considerations on the Right in Latin America." In Chalmers, do Carmo Campello de Souza, and Boron, *The Right and Democracy in Latin America*, 1–33.

Boschi, Renato R. "Empresarios y Sociedad en America Latina: La Herencia Estatal y Las Tradiciones Analiticas en un Marco de Cambios" (Business people and society in Latin America: State heritage and analytical traditions in a context of changes). In Tirado, *Los empresarios ante la globalización*, 30–44.

Brandes, Stuart D. *American Welfare Capitalism, 1880–1940*. Chicago: University of Chicago Press, 1976.

Brizzi, Adolfo, Natalia Gomez, and Matthew McMahon. "Agriculture and Rural Development." In Giugale, Lafourcade, and Luff, *Colombia*, 487–515.

Bruzzi Boechat, Claudio. Presentation at IDB Corporate Social Responsibility Conference, Salvador, Brazil. December 12, 2005.

Campello de Souza, Maria do Carmo. "The Contemporary Faces of the Brazilian Right: An Interpretation of Style and Substance." In Chalmers, do Carmo Campello de Souza, and Boron, *The Right and Democracy in Latin America*, 99–127.

Carrera, J., et al. *Estudio Exploratorio Responsabilidad Social Empresaria*, Red Puentes Argentina. Available at www.alianzas.org/archivos/documentos/RSEREDPUENTES.pps#1.

Caruso, Luis. "Xerox de Brasil y la Responsabilidad Social" (Xerox of Brazil and social responsibility). In Toro and Rey, *Empresa Privada y Responsabilidad Social*, 229–32.

Carvajalino, Guillermo. "La Fundación Corona." In Toro and Rey, *Empresa Privada y Responsabilidad Social*, 232–35.

Castañeda Ramos, Gonzalo. "Corporate Governance in Mexico." The Latin American Corporate Governance Roundtable, São Paulo, Brazil, April 26–28, 2000. Paris: OECD in cooperation with the World Bank Group, 2000. Available at www.oecd.org.

Catalan Torres, Luis. "Ley de Donaciones con Fines Culturales en Chile: Historia, Hechos, y Perfil de una Tension no Resuelta Entre Sociedad, Tercer Sector, y Estado" (Cultural donations law in Chile: History, facts, and profile of an unresolved tension among society, third sector, and state). Paper presented at the Third Meeting of the Latin American and Caribbean Network of ISTR, Buenos Aires, Argentina, September 2001.

CEDES. *Responsabilidad Social de las Empresas: Estudio sobre las actividades hacia la comunidad desarrolladas por empresas asociadas a la Cámara de*

Comercio de los Estados Unidos en Argentina. Buenos Aires: CEDES, 1998.

Cernea, Michael. "Farmer Organizations and Institution Building for Sustainable Development." *Regional Development Dialogue* 8, no. 2 (Summer 1987): 1–19.

Cerutti, Mario. *Propietarios, Empresarios, y Empresa en el Norte de Mexico* (Property owners, business people, and business in the north of Mexico). Mexico City: Siglo Veintiuno Editores, 2000.

Chalmers, Douglas A., Maria do Carmo Campello de Souza, and Atilio A. Boron, eds. *The Right and Democracy in Latin America.* New York: Praeger, 1992.

Chiquier, Loic. "Housing Finance." In Guigalek, Lafourcadek, and Luff, *Colombia,* 313–28.

Chudnovsky, Daniel, Bernardo Kosacoff, and Andres Lopez. *Las Multinacionales Latinoamericanas: Sus Estrategias en un Mundo Globalizado* [*Latinamerican multinationals: Their strategies in a globalizad world*]. Buenos Aires: Fondo de Cultura Economica, 1999.

Colsubsidio, *Informe y Balance General 2005.* Bogotá: Colsubsidio, 2006.

Corragio, J. L. "Prologo." In *De las Cofradías a las Organizaciones de la Sociedad Civi: Historia de la Iniciativa Asociativa en Argentina 1776–1990,* ed. R. Di Stefano. Buenos Aires: GADIS, 2002.

Coutinho, Rabelo. *Corporate Governance in Brazil.* Paris: OECD, 2001.

Crecía, M. J. *Integración de la RSE en la Estrategia Empresaria: Amanco Argentina y TNT Argentina.* Buenos Aires: Universidad de San Andrés, 2005.

Cruz, Luis Fernando. "La Experiencia de la Fundación Carvajal en el Desarrollo Social de Cali" [the experience of Fundación Carvajal in Cali's social development]. In Toro and Rey, *Empresa Privada y Responsabilidad Social,* 258–63.

Cuellar, Mauricio. "Transport." In Guigalek, Lafourcadek, and Luff, *Colombia,* 363–90.

Cuevas, Carlos, and Lisa Taber. "Rural Finance." In Giugale, Lafourcade, and Luff, *Colombia,* 587–607.

Cuevas, Mario Adolfo, Clemente Luis Del Valle, and Vicente Fretes Cibils. "Public Debt Sustainability and Management." In Giugale, Lafourcade, and Luff, *Colombia,* 193–254.

Dagnino, Evelina. "Os Movimentos Sociais e a emergência de uma Nova Cidadania." In *Anos 90: Política e Sociedade no Brasil,* ed. E. Dabnnino. São Paulo: Brasiliense, 1994. Quoted in Kisil, "Corporate Social Engagement and Corporate-Civil Society Partnership in Brazil."

De Cássia Guedes, Rita. "Responsabilidade Social and Cidadania Empresariais: Conceitos Estrategicos Para As Empresas Face a Globalização" (Corporate social responsibility and citizenship: Strategic concepts for businesses in globalization). Paper prepared for the Third Meeting of the Latin American and Caribbean Network of ISTR. Buenos Aires, Argentina, September 2001.

Defourny, Jacques, and Marthe Nyssens. "Defining Social Enterprise." In *Social Enterprise: At the Crossroads of Market, Public Policies, and Civil Society*, ed, Marthe Nyssens, 3–26. London: Routledge, 2006.

Díaz, Emilio Guerra. *IAF Corporate Social Engagement Project—Country Report: México*. Unpublished report, 2007.

Durand, Francisco. "From Fragile Crystal to Solid Rock: The Formation and Consolidation of a Business Association in Peru." In Bartell and Payne, *Business and Democracy in Latin America*, 141–78.

Durand, Francisco. *Incertidumbre y Soledad. Reflexiones Sobre los Grandes Empresarios de America Latina* [*Uncertainty and solitude, reflections on the big business people of Latin America*]. Lima: Fundación Friedrich Ebert, 1996.

———. "Las Organizaciones Empresariales Latinoamericanas el Final del Siglo XX" [Latin American business organizations at the end of the twentieth century). In Tirado, *Los empresarios ante la globalización*. 95–113.

———. "The New Right and Political Change in Peru." In Chalmers, do Carmo Campello de Souza, and Boron, *The Right and Democracy in Latin America*, 239–58.

Economist Intelligence Unit, "Argentina: Country Profile 2002." London, New York, Hong Kong: Economist Intelligence Unit, 2002. Available at www.eiu.com.

Economist, The. "How Good Should Your Business Be?" (January 19, 2008): 12–13.

———. "The Rich under Attack" (April 2, 2009).

Edwards, Sebastian. *The Economics and Politics of Transition to an Open Market Economy: Colombia*. Paris: OECD, 2001.

Elorrieta, Ana Maria. "Disclosure and Transparency: Accounting and Auditing." Paper presented at the Third Meeting of the Latin American Corporate Governance Roundtable, Mexico City, Mexico, April 8–10, 2002. Available at www.oecd.org.

Edwards, John K. "La Inversion Social, Una Decision Rentable" [Social investment, a profitable decision). In Toro and Rey, *Empresa Privada y Responsabilidad Social*, 236–39.

Farmelo, Martha. "How a Corporate Foundation Can Change the Way an NGO Does Business." Washington DC: IAF, n.d.

———. "Leading by Example: How to Institute CSR by Building Social Capital." Washington DC: IAF, n.d.

Feinberg, A. L. *La RSE como Consecuencia de Nuevas Formas de Autoridad Privada. Estudio Exploratorio sobre los Incentivos e Influencias que tienen las Empresas para Poder Adoptar Programas de Responsabilidad Social Empresaria*. Buenos Aires: Universidad de San Andrés, 2004.

Fisher, Julie. *The Road from Rio: Sustainable Development and the Nongovernmental Movement in the Third World*. Westport, CT: Praeger, 1993.

Fischer, Rosa Maria. "Intersectoral Alliances and the Reduction of Social Exclusion." In Sanborn and Portocarrero, *Philanthropy and Social Change in Latin America*, 135–62.

Fretes Cibils, Vicente, and Vicente Paqueo. "Enhancing Employment Opportunities through the Labor Markets." In Giugale, Lafourcade, and Luff, *Colombia*, 755–66.

Fundación Carvajal: A Social Enterprise. Available at www.carvajal.com.co website.

Gallup International. *Voice of the People: Opinion sobre RSE alrededor del mundo.* New York: Gallup International, 2004.

GDF. *Jornadas Internacionales GDF 2005 Hacia una vision estrategica de la inversion social.* Serie de Estudios de Inversion Social. Buenos Aires: GDF, 2005.

GDF. *Una aproximación al estudio de las fundaciones donantes en Argentina.* Buenos Aires: GDF, 2005.

Garsfield, Elsie, and Jairo Arboleda. "Violence, Sustainable Peace, and Development." In Giugale, Lafourcade, and Luff, *Colombia*, 35–58.

Gilchrest, George Bernard. "Fundación Mamonal." In Toro and Rey, *Empresa Privada y Responsabilidad Social*, 279–81.

Giovannucci, Daniele. "Coffee." In Giugale, Lafourcade, and Luff, *Colombia*, 517–57.

Giugale, Marcelo M. "Synthesis." In Giugale, Lafourcade, and Luff, *Colombia* 1–32.

Giugale, Marcelo M., Olivier Lafourcade, and Connie Luff, eds. *Colombia: The Economic Foundation of Peace.* Washington DC: The World Bank, 2003.

Giving USA 2005. Indianapolis: Giving USA Foundation, 2005.

Gomez Figari, Jaime. "Propal, El Papel de Desarrollo Social" (Propal, the role of social development). In Toro and Rey, *Empresa Privada y Responsabilidad Social*, 240–45.

Grajew, Oded, and Ricardo Young. "Manifesto for Sustainable Development." Instituto Ethos [2006].

Grayson, David, and Adrian Hodges. "Grupo Bimbo—Baking with Microfinance in Mexico." *Ethical Corporation* (December 14, 2006).

GrupoNueva. *Annual Report* (2007).

Guardans Carbo, Rafael. "El Reto Empresarial Para Alcanzar el Desarrollo Sostenido" (The corporate challenge to achieve sustainable development). In Toro and Rey, *Empresa Privada y Responsabilidad Social*, 250–57.

Gutierrez, Paola. "Transparencia, Fluidez, Integridad, y Revalacion de Informacion" (Transparency, fluidity, integrity, and revealing information). Presentation at the Third Meeting of the Latin American Corporate Governance Roundtable, São Paulo, Brazil, OECD in cooperation with the World Bank Group. April 8–10, 2002. Available at www.oecd.org.

Gutiérrez, Roberto. "Forces at the Macro and Micro Levels: Colombia." Unpublished report, 2009.

Gutiérrez, Roberto, Iván Darío Lobo, Diana M. Trujillo. "Corporate Social Engagement in Colombia." Unpublished report, 2007.

Haber, Stephan, ed. *Crony Capitalism and Economic Growth in Latin America.* Stanford, CA: Hoover Institution Press, 2002.

Helfand, Steven M. "The Political Economy of Agricultural Policy in Brazil: Decision Making and Influence from 1964 to 1992." *Latin American Research Review* 34, no. 2 (1999): 3–41. Available at www.jstor.org.

Heredia, Blanca. "Mexican Business and the State: The Political Economy of a Muddled Transition." In Bartell and Payne, *Business and Democracy in Latin America,* 179–216.

Heredia, Blanca. "Profits, Politics, and Size: The Political Transformation of Mexican Business." In Chalmers, do Carmo Campello de Souza, and Boron, *The Right and Democracy in Latin America,* 277–302.

Hirschman, Albert O. *Getting Ahead Collectively.* New York: Pergamon Press, 1984.

Hocol. "Postura Politics." Cited in Toro and Pineda-Londoño, "Philanthropy and Social Justice."

Hocol. *Sustainability Report 2005.* Bogotá, Colombia: Hocol, 2005.

Holm-Nielsen, Lauritz. "Higher Education." In Giugale, Lafourcade, and Luff, *Colombia,* 737–47.

Hustad, Bryan W., and Carlos Serrano. "Corporate Governance in Mexico." *Journal of Business Ethics* 37 (May 2002): 337–48. Available online.

IAF (Inter-American Foundation). *Fiscal Year 1999 Active Grants Results Report.* Washington DC: IAF, 1999.

IAPG. *Actividades comunitarias de la industria del Petróleo y del Gas.* Buenos Aires: IAPG, 2001.

———. *La Responsabilidad Social de las Empresas de la industria del Petróleo y del Gas.* Buenos Aires: IAPG, 2004.

IPEA (Instituto de Pesquisa Econômica Aplicada). *A Iniciativa Privada e o Espirito Publico* (Private initiative and public spirit). Brasilia: IPEA, 2002. Available at www.ipea.gov.br.

———. *A Iniciativa Privada e o Espírito Público: A evolução da ação social das emresas privadas no Brasil.* Brasilia: IPEA, 2006.

Instituto Ethos, "Ethos Indicators." 2001 edition. São Paulo, Brazil: Instituto Ethos, June, 2001. Available at www.ethos.org.br.

———. *Perfil Social, Racial, e de Genero das Directores de Grandes Empresas Brasileiras* (Social, racial, and gender profile of the directors of large Brazilian companies). São Paulo: Instituto Ethos, January 2002. Available at www.ethos.org.br.

———. *Ethos Indicators: ETHOS Corporate Social Responsibility Indicators.* São Paulo: Instituto Ethos, 2003.

———. "Responsabilidade Social das Empresas—Percepção do Consumidor Brasileiro, Pesquisa 2002" (Corporate social responsibility—perception of the Brazilian consumer, 2002 survey). São Paulo, Brazil: Instituto Ethos, 2002. Available at www.ethos.org.br.

Instituto Wal-Mart. 2007. Available at www.comunique-se.com.br/produtos/saladeimprensa/walmartpelacrianca_2006/instituto_walmart.htm.

Irrarázaval, Ignacio. *The New Alliance for Progress: Emerging Patterns of Business Social Engagement in Latin America—The Case of Chile.* Unpublished report, 2007.

Isgut, Alberto E. "What's Different about Exporters? Evidence from Colombian Manufacturing." *Journal of Development Studies* 37, no. 5 (June 2001): 57–82.

James, Kellee. "How CSR and an Entrepreneurial Business Culture Go Hand-in-Hand." Washington DC: IAF, n.d.

Jaramillo, Constanza, and Juan Alejandro Angel. "Responsabilidad Social Empresarial en Colombia: Resultado de una Investigación" (Corporate social responsibility in Colombia: Results of a study). In Toro and Rey, *Empresa Privada y Responsabilidad Social*, 246–49.

Jimenez, Miguel. "Global Change, Economic Restructuring and Labour Market Issues in Mexico City." *International Journal of Manpower* 21, no. 8 (2000): 464–80. Available at gessler.emeraldinsight.com.

Kadushin, Charles, and Lynda St. Clair. "Institutionalizing Community Action in Corporate America." In Tichy, McGill, and St. Clair, *Corporate Global Citizenship: Doing Business in the Public Eye*, 75–100.

Kanter, Rosabeth Moss, and Ricard Reisen de Pinho. *ABN-AMRO REAL: Banking on Sustainability.* Cambridge: Harvard Business School, October 25, 2005.

Katz, Jorge. "Structural Change and Labor Productivity Growth in Latin American Manufacturing Industries 1970–96." *World Development* 28, no. 9 (September 2000): 1583–96.

Kennedy, President John F. Speech on the occasion of the announcement of the Alliance for the Americas, March 1961. Available at en.wikipedia.org/wiki/Alliance_for_Progress.

Kingstone, Peter R. *Crafting Coalitions for Reform: Business Preferences, Political Institutions, and Neoliberal Reform in Brazil.* University Park: University of Pennsylvania Press, 1999.

Kisil, Marcos. "Corporate Social Engagement and Corporate-Civil Society Partnership in Brazil." Unpublished report, 2006.

———. "Update on CSR and the Economic Crisis: Brazil." Unpublished report, 2009.

Klabin. *Relatório de Sustenabilidade.* São Paolo: Klabin, 2006.

Landim, Leilah, Neide Beres, Regina List, and Lester M. Salamon. "Brasil." In Salamon et al., *Global Civil Society: Dimensions of the Nonprofit Sector.*

Laser Procianoy, Jairo. "Brazil: Company Partnership Models," *International Review of Financial-Analysis* 10, no. 3 (2001): 307–22. Available at www.sciencedirect.com.

Lawson, Philip. *The East India Company: A History.* New York: Longman, 1993.

Levinger, Beryl, and Jean McLeod. *Togetherness: How Government, Corporations, and NGOs Partner to Support Sustainable Development in Latin America.* Thematic Studies series. Arlington, VA: IAF, 2002.

Levy, Reynold. *Give and Take: A Candid Account of Corporate Philanthropy.* Cambridge: Harvard, MA Business School Press, 1999.

Lewis, John P. "Strengthening the Poor: Some Lessons for the International Community." In *Strengthening the Poor: What Have We Learned?* ed. John P. Lewis, 3–26. New Brunswick: Transaction Books, 1987.

Loeza, Soledad. "The Role of the Right in Political Change in Mexico, 1982–1988." In Chalmers, do Carmo Campello de Souza, and Boron, *The Right and Democracy in Latin America,* 128–41.

Luna, Elma. "La Filantropia Empresaria en Argentina." In *Fondos Privados Fines Públicos. El Empresariado y el Financiamiento de la Iniciativa Social en América Latina,* edited by Elma Luna. Buenos Aires: Espacio Editorial, GADIS, 1995.

Luna, Elma, and R. Serrano. "Introducción," in GADIS, *Directorio de Fundaciónes Empresarias Argentinas. Fondos Privados Fines Públicos,* Document series no. 4. Buenos Aires: GADIS, 1994.

Macario, Carla. "The Behavior of Manufacturing Firms under the New Economic Model," *World Development* 28, no. 9 (September 2000): 1597–1610.

Martin, Gary. "Employment and Unemployment in Mexico in the 1990s." *Monthly Labor Review* 123, no. 11 (November 2000): 3–19.

Mazar, Barnett, M. *Factores de Éxito en los Programas de Voluntariado Corporativo.* Buenos Aires: Universidad de San Andrés, 2005.

Milman, Claudio D., James P. D'Mello, Bulent Aybar, and Harvey Arbelaez. "On Using Mergers and Acquisitions to Gain Competitive Advantage in the United States in the Case of Latin American MNCS." *International Review of Financial-Analysis* 10, no. 3 (2001): 323–32.

Molino, Fernando. "Aspectos Tributarios de las Empresas de Inversion Social" (Aspects of taxation of social investment for businesses). In Toro and Rey, *Empresa Privada y Responsabilidad Social,* 178–81.

Montero Casassus. "Las Transformaciones a Nivel de la Empresa. Tendencias Organizacionales de la Reconversion en America Latina" (Transformations at the level of the firm: Organizational tendencies of the reconversion in Latin America). In Tirado, *Los empresarios ante la globalización,* 114–32.

Moreno, J. L. *La Política Social antes de la Política Social: Caridad, Beneficencia y Politica Social en Buenos Aires, Siglos XVII a XX.* Buenos Aires: Trama Editorial/Prometeo Libros, 2000.

Mortimore, Michael. "Corporate Strategies for FDI in the Context of Latin America's New Economic Model." *World Development* 28, no. 9 (September 2000): 1611–26.

Mortimore, Michael, and Wilson Peres. "Corporate Competitiveness in Latin America and the Caribbean." *CEPAL Review* 74 (August 2001): 35–57. Available at www.eclac.cl.

Nylen, William R. "Liberalism Para Todo Mundo, Menos Eu: Brazil and the Neoliberal Solution." In Chalmers, do Carmo Campello de Souza, and Boron, *The Right and Democracy in Latin America,* 259–76.

O'Donnell, Guillermo. "Substantive or Procedural Consensus? Notes on the Latin American Bourgeoisie." In Chalmers, do Carmo Campello de Souza, and Boron. *The Right and Democracy in Latin America*, 43–47.

OECD (Organization for Economic Co-operation and Development). "Policy Brief: Economic Survey of Mexico, 2002," *OECD Observer* (March 2002). Available at www.oecd.org.

———. *The Welfare State in Crisis*. Paris: OECD, 1989.

Paladino, M., ed. *Responsabilidad de la Empresa en la Sociedad*. Buenos Aires: Ariel, 2005.

Paladino, M., and A. Mohan. *Tendencias de Responsabilidad Social en Argentina*. Documento de Investigación. Buenos Aires: IAE/Universidad Austral, Aces, Pilar, 2002.

Partow, Zeinab. "Macroeconomic and Fiscal Frameworks." In Giugale, Lafourcade, and Luff, *Colombia*, 145–72.

PASCA. *Tax Incentives and Obstacles for Corporate Philanthropy in Venezuela, Mexico, Colombia, and Brazil, 2003*. Available at drclas .fas.harvard.edu/programs/PASCA/text/english/legal _engtxt.html.

Payne, Leigh A. "Brazilian Business and the Democratic Transition: New Attitudes and Influence." In Bartell and Payne, *Business and Democracy in Latin America*, 217–56.

Payne, Leigh A., and Ernest Bartell. "Bringing Business Back In: Business-State Relations and Democratic Stability in Latin America." In Bartell and Payne, *Business and Democracy in Latin America*, 258–76.

Penido de Freitas, Maria Christina, and Daniela Magalhães Prates. "Financial Openness: The Experience of Argentina, Brazil, and Mexico." *CEPAL Review* 70 (April 2000): 55–72. Available at www.eclac.cl.

Peres, Wilson, and Giovanni Stumpo. "Small and Medium-Sized Manufacturing Enterprises in Latin America and the Caribbean under the New Economic Model." *World Development* 28, no. 9 (September 2002): 1643–55.

Perrone, M. E. *Negocios en la Base de la Pirámide. Soluciones de Negocio para la Reducción de la Pobreza. Argentina: Prestación de Servicios a Sectores Pobres. El Caso de Aguas Argentinas, Gas Natural Ban y Movistar*. Buenos Aires: Universidad de San Andrés, 2005.

Pollner, John. "The Financial Sector." In Giugale, Lafourcade, and Luff, *Colombia*, 255–77.

Porter, Michael E., and Mark R. Kramer. "The Competitive Advantage of Corporate Philanthropy." *Harvard Business Review* (December 2002): 5–16.

———. "Strategy and Society: The Link between Competitive Advantage and Corporate Social Responsibility." *Harvard Business Review* (December 2006): 78–93.

Portocarrero S., Felipe, Cynthia Sanborn, Sergio Llusera, and Viviana Quea. *Empresas, Fundaciones, y Medios: La Responsabilidad Social en el Peru*

(Businesses, foundations, and the media: Social responsibility in Peru). Lima: Centro de Investigacion de la Universidad del Pacifico, 2000.

Pralahad, C. K. *The Fortune at the Bottom of the Pyramid: Eradicating Poverty through Profits.* Philadelphia: Wharton School Press, 2004.

Procura, A. C. "Empresas y Empresarios: Tendencias Actuales de la Filantropia Corporativa en México" (Businesses and business people: Contemporary tendencies in corporate philanthropy in Mexico). Paper presented at the Third Annual Conference of the International Society of Third Sector Research, July 2001.

————. "Movilizacion de Recursos para la Responsabilidad Social Empresarial" (Mobilization of resources for corporate social responsibility). Paper presented at the Third Annual Conference of the International Society of Third Sector Research, July 2001.

Puppim de Oliveira, J. A., and M. A. Gardetti. "Analysing Changes to Prioritise Corporate Citizenship: The Case of Sustainability in Perez-Companc, Argentina." *Journal of Corporate Citizenship* (Spring 2006): 71–83.

Queiroz, Adele, and Vivian Paes Barretto Smith. "Indicadores de Responsabilidade Social Empresarial: Como o Tereiro Setor Contribui Para a Melhoria de Atuação Social Empresarial." ([How the third sector contributes to the improvement of corporate social performance]. Paper presented at the Third Meeting of the Latin American and Caribbean Network of the ISTR, Buenos Aires, Argentina, September 2001.

Qureshi, Moeen A. "The World Bank and NGOs: New Approaches." Paper presented at the Washington chapter of the Society for International Development conference entitled "Learning from the Grassroots," April 1988.

Rabelo, Flavio Marcilio, and Luciano Coutinho. "Corporate Governance in Brazil." Paper presented at the Policy Dialogue Meeting on Corporate Governance in Developing Countries and Emerging Economies, OECD Headquarters, Paris. Organization for Economic Co-operation and Development, OECD Development Center, April 2001. Available at www.oecd.org.

Reinhardt, Nola, and Wilson Peres. "Latin America's New Economic Model: Micro Responses and Economic Restructuring." *World Development* 28, no. 9 (September 2000): 1543–66.

Renato Souza, Paulo. "Education and Development in Brazil, 1995–2000," *CEPAL Review* 73 (April 2001): 65–80. Available at www.eclac.cl.

Restrepo, Maria Inez. "Caja de Compensacion Familiar—COMFAMA." In Toro and Rey, *Empresa Privada y Responsabilidad Social,* 284–85.

Restrepo, Margarita Inez. "Corporacion Antoquia Presente." In Toro and Rey, *Empresa Privada y Responsabilidad Social,* 276–78.

Ritchey-Vance, Marion. *The Art of Association: NGOs and Civil Society in Colombia.* Arlington, VA: IAF, 1991.

Roitstein, F. *La Responsibilidad Social Empresarial en la Argentina: Tendencias y Oportunidades.* Buenos Aires: Instituto Universitario IDEEA, Documentos de Investigación, 2003.

Roitter, Mario M. "La Nocion del Buen Vecino y la Construccion de Ciudadania Empresaria: Convergencia o Divergencia con Tendencias Internacionales" (The notion of the good neighbor and the construction of corporate citizenship: Convergence or divergence with international tendencies). Paper presented at the Second Meeting of the Latin American and Caribbean Network of ISTR in Santiago, Chile, September 1999.

————. "La Razon Social de Las Empresas: Una Investigacion Sobre los Vinculos Entre Empresa y Sociedad en Argentina, Version Resumida" (The trade name/social rationale of companies: An investigation of the links between business and society in Argentina, condensed version). Document no. 115. Buenos Aires: CEDES, December 1996. Available at www.cedes.org.

Roitter, Mario, Regina List, and Lester M. Salamon. "Argentina." In Salamon et al., *Global Civil Society: Dimensions of the Nonprofit Sector.*

Roitter, Mario M., and M. Camerlo. "Corporate Social Action in a Context of Crisis: Reflections on the Argentine Case." In Sanborn and Portocarrero, *Philanthropy and Social Change in Latin America,* 223–51.

Rojas, Cristina, and Gustavo Morales. "Private Contributions to the Public Sphere." In Sanborn and Portocarrero, *Philanthropy and Social Change in Latin America,* 163–90.

Romero, Carlos, and Angel Maas. "Bimbo Group and Papalote Museo del Niño." Social Enterprise Knowledge Network. Unpublished case study. July 25, 2003.

Saez, Felipe. "Corruption, Institutional Performance, and Governance: Developing an Anticorruption Strategy for Colombia." In Giugale, Lafourcade, and Luff, *Colombia,* 931–55.

Salamon, Lester M. "The Rise of Nonprofit Organizations." *Foreign Affairs* 73, no. 4 (July/August 1994): 111–24.

Salamon, Lester M., Helmut K. Anheier, Regina List, Stefan Toepler, S. Wojciech Sokolowski, and Associates, eds. *La Sociedad Civil Global.* Bilboa: Fundación BBVA, 1999. Published in English as *Global Civil Society: Dimensions of the Nonprofit Sector.* Baltimore: Johns Hopkins Center for Civil Society Studies, 1999.

Sanborn, Cynthia. "Philanthropy in Latin America: Historical Traditions and Current Trends." In Sanborn and Portocarrero, *Philanthropy and Social Change in Latin America,* 3–29.

Sanborn, Cynthia, and Felipe Portocarrero, "Editors' Introduction." In Sanborn and Portocarrero, *Philanthropy and Social Change in Latin America,* xi–xx.

————, eds. *Philanthropy and Social Change in Latin America.* Cambridge, MA: David Rockefeller Center Series on Latin American Studies, Harvard University, 2005.

Sanborn, Cynthia, Hanny Cueva, Felipe Portocarrero, Regina List, and Lester M. Salamon. "Peru." In Salamon et al., *Global Civil Society: Dimensions of the Nonprofit Sector.*

Sangines, Mario F., and Eduardo Fernandez. "Budgetary Institutions." In Giugale, Lafourcade, and Luff, *Colombia,* 981–94.

Santiago Reyes, and Miguel Angel. "Ecopetrol y Sus Relaciones con la Comunidad" (Ecopetrol and its relationship with the community). In Toro and Rey, *Empresa Privada y Responsabilidad Social,* 267–74.

Schamis, Hector E. "Conservative Political Economy in Latin America and Western Europe: The Political Sources of Privatization." In Chalmers, do Carmo Campello de Souza, and Boron, *The Right and Democracy in Latin America,* 48–67.

Schneider, Ben Ross. "Privatization in the Collor Government: Triumph of Liberalism or Collapse of the Developmental State?" In Chalmers, do Carmo Campello de Souza, and Boron, *The Right and Democracy in Latin America,* 225–38.

Silva, Eduardo. *The State and Capital in Chile: Business Elites, Technocrats, and Market Economics.* Boulder, CO: Westview Press, 1996.

Sims, Ronald. *Ethics and Corporate Social Responsibility.* New York: Praeger, 2003.

Smith, Craig. "The New Corporate Philanthropy." *Harvard Business Review* 72, no. 1 (May/June 1994): 105–16.

Tanski, Janet M., and Dan W. French. "Capital Concentration and Market Power in Mexico's Manufacturing Industry: Has Trade Liberalization Made a Difference?" *Journal of Economic Issues* 35, no. 3 (September 2000): 1689–1702.

Teixido, Soledad, Reinalina Chavarri, and Andrea Castro. "La Responsabilidad Social Empresarial en Chile: Innovacion y Desafios" (Social responsibility in Chile: Innovation and challenges). Paper prepared for presentation at the Third Meeting of the Latin American and Caribbean Network of the ISTR, Buenos Aires, Argentina, September 2001.

Tercer Sector. "Revisión de ejemplares desde 2002 hasta 2006. Selección de artículos que ilustran casos o puntos de vista teóricos." *Tercer Sector.* 2006.

Tichy, Noel M., Andrew R. McGill, and Lynda St. Clair, eds. *Corporate Global Citizenship: Doing Business in the Public Eye.* San Francisco: The New Lexington Press, 1997.

Tirado, Ricardo. "La Vision del Cambio de los Grandes Empresarios" (Vision of change of the major business people]. In Tirado, *Los empresarios ante la globalización.*

———, ed. *Los empresarios ante la globalización* (Business people and globalization). Mexico City: Instituto de Investigaciones Legislativas, Camara de Diputados del H. Congreso de la Union and La Universidad Nacional Autonoma de Mexico, la Division de Investigaciones Sociales, 1994.

Toro, Olga Lucia, and German Rey, eds. *Empresa Privada y Responsabilidad Social* (Private business and social responsibility). Bogotá: Utopica Ediciones, 1996.

Toro, Olga Lucia, and Natalia Pineda-Londoño. "Philanthropy and Social Justice in the Andes: The Case of Hocol S.A. and Fundación Hocol." Unpublished paper, June 2004.

UN (United Nations). *Global Outlook 2000: An Economic, Social, and Environmental Perspective.* New York: UN, 1990.

US Department of State, Bureau of Economic and Business Affairs. "Argentina"; "Brazil"; "Colombia"; "Mexico"; "Peru"; and "Venezuela." 2001 Country Reports on Economic Policy and Trade Practices (February 2002). All available at www.state.gov/e/eb/rls/rpts/eptp/2001/wha/.

Uphoff, Norman. "Assisted Self-Reliance: Working with, Rather than for, the Poor." In Lewis, *Strengthening the Poor*, 47–60.

Uvalle Berrones, R. "La Gerencia Social: Una Opción de Gobierno Abierto." *Estudio Político*, no. 4 (July/December 1993).

Valencia, Oscar Giraldo. "Corporacion de Accion Solidaria—CORPOSOL." In Toro and Rey, *Empresa Privada y Responsabilidad Social*, 282–83.

Velez, Eduardo. "Education." In Giugale, Lafourcade, and Luff, *Colombia*, 611–51.

Verduzco, Gustavo, Regina List, and Lester M. Salamon. "Mexico." In Salamon et al., *Global Civil Society: Dimensions of the Nonprofit Sector.*

Vidal, Eloy. "Information and Communications Technology Sector." In Giugale, Lafourcade, and Luff, *Colombia*, 421–32.

Viguera, Anibal. "Los Empresarios, La Politica, y Las Politicas en America Latina. Una Propuesta de Analisis Comparado" (Business people, policy, and politics in Latin America. A Proposal of comparative analysis). In Tirado, *Los empresarios ante la globalización*, 76–94.

Villar, Rodrigo, Regina List, and Lester M. Salamon. "Colombia." In Salamon et al., *Global Civil Society: Dimensions of the Nonprofit Sector.*

Vives, Antonio, and Estrella Peinado-Vara. *Corporate Social Responsibility as a Tool for Competitiveness: Proceedings. Inter-American Conference on Corporate Social Responsibility, Panama City, October 26–28, 2003.* Washington DC: IDB, 2004.

———. "Introduction: Deeds Not Words." In *Corporate Social Responsibility: Deeds Not Words: Proceedings. II Inter-American Conference on Social Responsibility, Mexico City, September 26–28, 2004.* Washington DC: IDB, n.d. [2005].

Vogel, David. *The Market for Virtue: The Potential and Limits of Corporate Social Responsibility.* Washington DC: Brookings Institution Press, 2005.

Wal-Mart Brazil. "Brazil Sustainability Strategy." PowerPoint presentation. January 10, 2007. Brazil: Wal-Mart Brazil, 2007.

Weller, Jurgen. "Employment Trends in Latin America and the Caribbean During the 1990s." *CEPAL Review* 72 (December 2000): 31–52. Available at www.eclac.cl.

Weyland, Kurt. "Economic Policy in Chile's New Democracy." *Journal of Interamerican Studies and World Affairs* 41, no. 3 (September 1999): 67–96.

Wiebe, Robert H. *Businessmen and Reform: A Study of the Progressive Movement.* Cambridge: Harvard University Press, 1962.

World Bank. *Brazil Higher Education Sector Survey, Volume I.* Report no. 19392–BR. June 30, 2000. Available at www.worldbank.org.

———. *Mexico. Export Dynamics and Productivity: Analysis of Mexican Manufacturing in the 1990s.* September 15, 2000. Available at www.worldbank.org.

———. *Small and Medium-Sized Enterprises in Argentina. A Potential Engine for Economic Growth and Employment.* Report no. 22803–AR. August 2002. Available at www.worldbank.org.

World Business Council for Sustainable Development. *Corporate Social Responsibility: Making Good Business Sense.* Conches-Geneva, Switzerland: WBCSD, 2000.

Zunz, Olivier. *Making America Corporate.* Chicago: University of Chicago Press, 1990.

Zolezzi, Eduardo. "Energy Sector Strategy." In Giugale, Lafourcade, and Luff, *Colombia,* 391–419.

Personal Interviews

Unless otherwise indicated, interviews were conducted by the author.

Abogabir, Ximena. President, Masisa. Personal interview by Jens Prinzhorn. Santiago, Chile. June 5, 2007.

Adaro, Daniel. 2007. Mayor of Antofagasta. Personal interview by Jens Prinzhorn. Antofagasta, Chile. June 7, 2007.

Aguiar, Sele. Arcor Corporation. Presentation at the IV Inter-American Development Bank Conference on CSR. Salvador, Brazil. December 11, 2006.

Altamirano Hernandez, Gabriel. Director, Fundación Televisa. Mexico City, Mexico. May 10, 2005.

Andrigueto, Juliana. General Coordinator, Holcim. Personal interview by Jens Prinzhorn. São Paulo, Brazil. June 12, 2007.

Arango Arias, Manuel. President and CEO, Concorde, S.A., DE, C.V. Mexico. October 17, 2005.

Arcanjo, Ricardo. President, Associação Comercial e Industrial de Telêmaco Borba, Klabin. Personal interview by Jens Prinzhorn. Telêmaco Borba, Brazil. June 18, 2007.

Arenas-Wightman, Wendy. Executive Director, AVINA Foundation Colombia. Bogotá, Colombia. November 10, 2006.

Aurelio da Silva, Marco. Head of Associação Ortópolis Barroso, Holcim. Personal interview by Jens Prinzhorn. Barroso, Brazil. June 14, 2007.

Ausderau, Karen. Social Management Analyst, Hocol. Personal interview by Jens Prinzhorn. Bogotá, Colombia. June 21, 2007.

Aylwin Oyarzún, Francisco. Executive Director, Fundación Telefonica. Santiago, Chile. May 2, 2006.

Batista da Silva, Marlene. Social Assistant, Klabin. Personal interview by Jens Prinzhorn. Telêmaco Borba, Brazil. June 18, 2007.

Bennett Olivares, Lucy. Chief, Institutional Relations, Telefonica/ CTC Chile, Compañia de Telecomunicaciones de Chile, S.A. Santiago, Chile. May 2, 2006.

Berger, Gabriel. Telephone interview. August 10, 2009.

Bernal Hadad, Camilo. Rector General, Uniminuto. Bogotá, Colombia. November 10, 2006.

Bolivar Garcia, Maria Del Pilar. Director of Organization Communication, Alpina. Bogotá, Colombia. November 9, 2006.

Breslin, Pat. Inter-American Foundation. Washington DC. August 3, 2005.

Cabrera, Nury. Owner of canteen in San Francisco, Colombia. Personal interview by Jens Prinzhorn. San Francisco, Colombia. June 22, 2007.

Cabrera, Vianney. Head of kiosk supported through Hocol's micro-credit program. Personal interview by Jens Prinzhorn. San Francisco, Colombia. June 22, 2007.

Caravedo Molinari, Baltazar. Executive Director, AVINA/Peru. Lima, Peru. March 25, 2004.

Carvalho Pinto, Cristina. President, Jazz de Comunicação. São Paulo, Brazil. December 14, 2006.

Cardenas Zacarias, Oralia. SEDAC. Ixmiquilpan, Mexico. October 21, 2005.

Castro Benetti, Diana. AVINA. Bogotá, Colombia. November 10, 2006.

Contreras, Francisco. Head of Communication, Fundación Minera Escondida. Personal interview by Jens Prinzhorn. Antofagasta, Chile. June 7, 2007.

Comelli, Silvana. Director of Social Development, Minetti. Buenos Aires, Argentina. May 9, 2007.

Cordery Duprat, Carla. Social Investment Director, PMV. São Paulo, Brazil. December 14, 2006.

Correa Guzman, Pedro. Gerente de Asuntos Corporativos. Fundación Minera Escondida. Antofagasta, Chile. June 7, 2007.

Correa, Maria Emilia. Manager of Social and Environmental Responsibility, Masisa. Personal interview by Jens Prinzhorn. Santiago, Chile. June 5, 2007.

Cuéllar Cabrera, Juan Manuel. Lawyer/External Relations Team, Hocol. Personal interview by Jens Prinzhorn. Bogotá, Colombia. June 21, 2007.

da Graça Marson Cella, Maria. Director, Escola Estadual Luiz Vieira, Klabin. Personal interview by Jens Prinzhorn. Telémaco Borba, Brazil. June 18, 2007.

das Gracas Oliveira, Maria. Presidente de la Cocina Comun., Holcim. Personal interview by Jens Prinzhorn. Barroso, Brazil. June 15, 2007.

de Fiori, Daniela. Instituto Wal-Mart. Personal interview by Jens Prinzhorn. São Paolo, Brazil. June 13, 2007.

de Mello Neto, Wilson Newton. Vice President, Wal-Mart Brazil. Presentation at IV Inter-American Conference on Corporate Social Responsibility. Salvador, Brazil. December 12, 2006.

De Oliveira Pinto, Maria Luiza. Sustainability Director, ABN-Amro Bank. São Paolo, Brazil. December 13, 2006.

de Oliveria Neto, Valdemar (Moneto). Brazil Representative, AVINA. Budapest, Hungary. June 6, 2005.

do Vale, José Mauricio. Representative, Centro de Promoçao Humana de Telêmaco Borba, Klabin. Personal interview by Jens Prinzhorn. Telêmaco Borba, Brazil. June 16, 2007.

Dussan Medina, Salvador. Farmer and land owner in San Francisco, Colombia. Personal interview by Jens Prinzhorn. San Francisco, Colombia. June 22, 2007.

Estevez Valencia, Francisco. Director, Division of Social Organizations, Ministry of the Secretary General of the Government. Santiago, Chile. May 5, 2006.

Favaretto, Sonia. Executive Director, Bank Boston Foundation. São Paolo, Brazil. September 29, 2002.

Fernandez, Reubem. Vice Chairman, Colombian Confederation of NGOs, Bogotá, Colombia. November 7, 2006.

Ferrarezi, Elizabete. Council of Social Solidarity. São Paolo, Brazil. September 28, 2002.

Ferreira, Lúcia. Presidente del Grupo de las Madres, Holcim. Personal interview by Jens Prinzhorn. Barroso, Brazil. June 14, 2007.

Fleury, Ciro. Executive Director, IQE. São Paulo, Brazil. December 15, 2006.

Forero, Andres. Technical Manager, Microsoft. Personal interview by Jens Prinzhorn. Bogotá, Colombia. November 8, 2006.

Forero, Consuelo. Vice President of the Micro Credit Committee, Hocol. Personal interview by Jens Prinzhorn. San Francisco, Colombia. June 22, 2007.

Garcia Angulo, Salvador. Executive Director, SEDAC. Ixmiquilpan, Mexico. October 21, 2005.

German-Phinder, Klaus. Ganar-Ganar Magazine. Mexico City, Mexico. October 20, 2005.

Giomi, Claudio. Director of CSR, Arcor. Buenos Aires, Argentina. May 10, 2007.

Gómez, Istar Jimena. Empresarios por la Educación. Bogotá, Colombia. November 9, 2006.

Gómez, Mauricio. Executive Director, MEPE/ExE. Personal interview by Jens Prinzhorn. Bogotá, Colombia. June 20, 2007.

Gonzalez Esparza, Juan Alberto. Director, Andean Region, Microsoft. Bogotá, Colombia. November 7, 2006.

Gorleri, Constanza. Director of External Relations, Banco Galicia. Buenos Aires. Argentina. May 8, 2007.

Grajew, Oded. Founder, Instituto Ethos. Salvador, Brazil. December 12, 2006.

Grimm, Martha Del Rio. Director, Fundemex (Fundación del Empresario en Mexico). Mexico City, Mexico. October 18, 2005.

Gross, D., Felipe. Director of Social Programs, Hogar de Cristo. Santiago, Chile. May 3, 2006.

Gutiérrez Prieto, Eduardo. Assistant Director General, Corporacion Minuto de Dios. Bogotá, Colombia. November 9, 2006.

Gutiérrez, Roberto. Professor, Uni-Andes. Bogotá, Colombia. November 7, 2006.

Gutiérrez Sampedo, Jorge. Manager, Colsubsidio. Bogotá, Colombia. November 8, 2006.

Guzmán Gatica, Leon. Director General, ACCION/ RSE. Personal interview by Jens Prinzhorn. Santiago, Chile, May 3, 2006.

Guzmán, Pedro Correa. General Manager for Corporate Issues, Minera Escondida. Antofagasta, Chile. June 8, 2007.

Haddad, Sergio. Board Chairman, ABONG. São Paolo, Brazil. December 15, 2006.

Heitkoiter de Melo, Dalton A. President, Klabin. Personal interview by Jens Prinzhorn. Telêmaco Borba, Brazil. June 16, 2007.

Hernandez, Martha Eugenia. Vice President for Institutional Relations, Grupo Bimbo. Mexico City, Mexico. October 17, 2005.

Hernandez, Juan Emilio. Director, Office of Institutional Relations. Bogotá, Colombia. November 11, 2006.

Hernández-Vargas, Javier. Wal-Mart Mexico, Mexico City, Mexico. May 10, 2005.

Herrera Guerra, Ernesto. Director General, Reforestamos Mexico, A.C. Mexico City, Mexico. October 17, 2005.

Irarrázaval Llona, Ignacio. Vice Rector, Pontifica Universidad Católica de Chile. Santiago, Chile, May 5, 2006.

Itacarambi, Paulo. Executive Director, Instituto Ethos. São Paulo, Brazil. July 9, 2003.

Johannpeter, Jorge Gerdau. Gerdau Steel. Porto Allegre, Brazil. October 1, 2002.

Johannpeter, Maria Elena. Executive Director, Parceiras Voluntaríos. Porto Allegre, Brazil. October 1, 2002.

Jordan Quijano, Maria Catalina. Alpina. Bogotá, Colombia. November 9, 2006.

Kisil, Marcos. President, IDIS. São Paulo, Brazil. October 5, 2002; December 14, 2006; and December 16, 2006.

Kolko, Linda. Vice-president, IDB. January 25, 2005.

Lagos Weber, Ricardo. Minister, Ministry of the General Secretary of the Government. Santiago, Chile. May 4, 2006.

Leal, Guilherme Peirão. Co-President, Natura. Presentation to the IV Inter-American Conference on Corporate Social Responsibility. Salvador, Brazil. December 10, 2006.

Lebrija, Alicia. Director of Educational Development, Fundación Televisa. Mexico City, Mexico. May 10, 2005.

Lima, Wilberto Luíz, Jr., Communication and CSR Director, Klabin. São Paulo, Brazil. December 15, 2006.

———. Personal interview by Jens Prinzhorn. São Paulo, Brazil. June 12, 2007.

Linguette, Marcello. Instituto Ethos. São Paulo, Brazil. July 16, 2003.

Lio, Santos. Director, Arcor Foundation. Buenos Aires, Argentina. May 10, 2007.

Llapur, Maria Bettina. Executive Director, Gas Naturale Ban. Buenos Aires, Argentina. May 10, 2007.

Madrid-Varela, Carlos. Mexican Association of Fundraising Professionals. Mexico City, Mexico. May 10, 2005.

Maillé, Mauricio. Fundación Televisa. Mexico City, Mexico. May 10, 2005.

Manuel Cuéllar Cabrera, Juan. Abogado, Equipo Relaciones (Lawyer), Hocol. Personal interview by Jens Prinzhorn. Bogotá, Colombia. June 21, 2007.

Marlena Páez Gutiérrez, Betty. Executive Director, Hocol Foundation. Personal interview by Jens Prinzhorn. Neiva, Colombia. June 22, 2007.

Martin, Nicolas. Executive Director, Somas Más. Bogotá, Colombia. November 10, 2006.

Mindlin, Sérgio. CEO, Fundação Telefônica Foundation. São Paulo, Brazil. December 13, 2006.

Moncayo, Javier. Prodepaz. Bogotá, Colombia. November 7, 2006.

Montilla H., Maria Del Pilar. Director of Technical Cooperation, Fundación Social. Bogotá, Colombia. November 11, 2006.

Moraes, Gabriel. Social Coordinator Barroso, Holcim. Personal interview by Jens Prinzhorn. Barroso, Brazil. June 14, 2007.

Moreira Hudson, Agustin P., Presidente, Fondo Esperanza/Hogar de Cristo. Santiago, Chile. May 3, 2006.

Moura, Julio. Presentation at the IV Inter-American Conference on Corporate Social Responsibility. Salvador, Brazil. December 10, 2006. For information on the WBCSD, see www.wbcsd.org.

Mourão Fonseca, Rosimauro. Holcim. Personal interview by Jens Prinzhorn. Barroso, Brazil. June 15, 2007.

Noble, Giseal. Wal-Mart Mexico. Mexico City, Mexico. October 21, 2005.

Obregon, Pablo Gabriel. Chairman of the Board, Colombian Confederation of NGOs. Bogotá, Colombia. November 7, 2006.

Ojeda, Jose. Executive Director, Fundación Minera Escondida. Antofagasta, Chile. May 5, 2006.

Ojeda, José Miguel. Executive Director, Fundación Minera Escondida. Personal interview by Jens Prinzhorn. Santiago, Chile. June 7, 2007.

Ospina, Rosa Ines. Transparencia Internacional. Bogotá, Colombia. November 7, 2006.

Paschoal, Luis Norberto. President, Fundação Educar Paschoal. São Paulo, Brazil. December 13, 2006.

Peón Escalante, Fernando. Director General, Fomento Sociál Banamex. Mexico City, Mexico. May 11, 2005.

Pierce, Steve. IAF Field Representative for the Andes. Catagena, Colombia. January 25, 1995.

Ponce, Hernan. Institute for Development Planning. Ixmiquilpan, Mexico. October 20, 2005.

Price, Walter. Inter-American Foundation. Arlington, Virginia, August 3, 2005.

Ramírez Trujillo, Esperanza. Empresarios por la Educación. Bogotá, Colombia. November 10, 2006.

Raposa, Rebecca. President, GIFE. São Paolo, Brazil. October 3, 2002.

Reyes de Fuentes, Rhina. Director, Fundemas. Santiago, Chile. May 3, 2006.

Rosetti, Fernando. Executive Director, GIFE. São Paulo, Brazil. December 13, 2006.

Rojas-Gonzalez de Castilla, Susana. Director General, Pro-Natura. Mexico City, Mexico. October 20, 2005.

Ruiz, Emilia. Executive Director, Fundación Corona. Bogotá, Colombia. November 10, 2006.

Saldarriago Molina, P. Daniel. Banco De Alimentos. Bogotá, Colombia. November 10, 2006.

Salopera, Petri. Coordinator, Social Development Area, Fundación Minera Escondida. Antofagasta, Chile. May 5, 2006.

Sánchez, Antonio. Gerente de Desarrollo Gremial, Fundación Minera Escondida. Personal interview by Jens Prinzhorn. Antofagasta, Chile. June 8, 2007.

Santa, Ramiro. Stakeholder Value Team Leader, Hocol. Bogotá, Colombia. November 10, 2006.

Santa, Ramiro. Stakeholder Value Team Leader, Hocol. Personal interviews by Jens Prinzhorn. Bogotá, Colombia. November 11, 2006 and June 20, 2007.

Sarmiento Gomez, Diego. Coordinator of Operations, Microsoft Solidario. Bogotá, Colombia. November 7, 2006.

Sarnoski, Osvaldo. President, Associaçao Educacional Fanuel Guarda Mirim, Klabin. Personal interview by Jens Prinzhorn. Telêmaco Borba, Brazil. June 16, 2007.

Schlosser, Silvio José. Executive Director, Fundación YPF. Buenos Aires, Argentina. May 7, 2007.

Sérgio Ademar, Paulo. Head of the WG 3: Empreendedorismo difundido e implementado (Implementing and evaluating entrepreneurship initiatives), Holcim. Personal interview by Jens Prinzhorn. Barroso, Brazil. June 15, 2007.

Siegrist Prado, Jorge. Vice President for Communications and Public Relations, Grupo Modelo. Mexico City, Mexico. May 9, 2005.

Tapia de Múñoz, Guadalupe. Júnior Lague de la ciudad de Mexico. Mexico City, Mexico. October 18, 2005.

Tironi Valdivieso, Alejandra. SOFOFA. Santiago, Chile. May 4, 2006.

Toro, Bernardo. Adviser, Avina Foundation. Bogotá, Columbia. November 10, 2006.

Trespalacios Peñas, Alvaro. Director General, Corporacion Minuto de Dios. Bogotá, Colombia. November 9, 2006.

Valenzuela, Jaime. Fundación Minera Escondida. Personal interview by Jens Prinzhorn. Antofagasta, Chile. June 7, 2008.

Veloso Villarzu, Solange. Directora Social, Fundación Minera Escondida. Personal interview by Jens Prinzhorn. Antofagasta, Chile. June 8, 2007.

Vicuña P., Ricardo. Director of Statistical Information and Investigation, Central Bank of Chile. Santiago, Chile. May 2, 2006.

Villalobos, Jorge. Executive Director, CEMEFI. Mexico City, Mexico. May 9, 2005.

Villar, Rodrigo. Consultant, IAF. Alexandria, Virginia. August 3, 2005.

Voight, Leo. Presidente, GIFE. São Paolo, Brazil. September 28, 2002.

von Buettner, Edgar. Consultor Sênor em Planejamento Estratégico e Gestão Sistêma de Projectos (Strategic senior consultant), Holcim. Personal interview by Jens Prinzhorn. Barroso, Brazil. June 14, 2007.

Wood, Marcia. Associate, IDIS. Personal interview by Jens Prinzhorn. São Paulo, Brazil. July 3, 2007.

Young, Ricardo. President, Instituto Ethos. São Paulo, Brazil. December 14, 2006.

About the Author

Lester M. Salamon is a professor at the Johns Hopkins University and director of the Johns Hopkins Center for Civil Society Studies and of its Comparative Nonprofit Sector and Listening Post projects. Prior to this he served as director of the Center for Governance and Management Research at The Urban Institute and as deputy associate director of the U.S. Office of Management and Budget in the Executive Office of the President. Dr. Salamon received his Ph.D. in government from Harvard University and his B.A. in policy studies from Princeton University. He is the author of, among other works, *Partners in Public Service: Government-Nonprofit Relations in the Modern Welfare State* (Johns Hopkins University Press, 1996); *Defining the Nonprofit Sector* (Manchester University Press, 1997), *The Tools of Government: A Guide to the New Governance* (Oxford University Press, 2002), *The State of Nonprofit America* (Brookings Institution Press, 2002), *The Resilient Sector* (Brookings Institution Press, 2003), and *Global Civil Society: Dimensions of the Nonprofit Sector* (Kumarian Press, 2004). Dr. Salamon received the 2003 Distinguished Leadership Award from the Association for Research on Nonprofit Organizations and Voluntary Action for his work on the nonprofit sector in the United States and abroad. He is past chairman of the board of the Community Foundation of Anne Arundel County and serves on the editorial boards of *Voluntas, Administration and Society, Nonprofit and Voluntary Action Quarterly,* and on the Scientific Committee of *Atlantide.*

Index

*Kumarian Press, located in Sterling, Virginia, is a forward-looking,
scholarly press that promotes active international engagement and
an awareness of global connectedness.*